A Guide for Culturally Responsive Teaching in Adult Prison Educational Programs

A Guide for Culturally Responsive Teaching in Adult Prison Educational Programs

Michael Gray

To order additional copies of this book, contact:
Xlibris
1-888-795-4274
www.Xlibris.com
Orders@Xlibris.com
566520

TABLE OF CONTENTS

ACKNOWLEDGMENTS xi

Chapter

1. INTRODUCTION

    Background 1

    Purpose of the Project 9

    Definition of Terms 11

    Limitations 13

    Significance of the Project 14

    Organization of the Remainder of the Project 15

2. REVIEW OF THE RELATED LITERATURE

    Introduction 16

    Correctional Institutions Teaching and Management Conditions...17

    Culturally Responsive Teaching 29

    Learning Theory 40

        Motivation 44

    Rationale 50

    Summary 51

3. METHODODLOGY

    Research Design 56

Setting of the Project 57

Population and Sample 58

Data Collection 60

Data Analysis 61

Analysis of Data 61

Findings 69

Interpretation 71

Description of the Project 75

Summary 76

4. SUMMARY, CONCLUSIONS AND RECOMMENDATIONS

Summary 80

Conclusions 89

Recommendations 91

APPENDICES

A. Human Subjects Approval Review Forms 95

B. Interview Protocol 103

C. The Project: Culturally Responsive Teaching in Adult

Prisons: An Educational Program 108

References 125

Abstract

of

A GUIDE FOR CULTURALLY RESPONSIVE TEACHING

IN ADULT PRISON EDUCATIONAL PROGRAMS

by

Michael Gray

Brief Review of Literature

Increasingly, prison education programs are multicultural environments where teachers must relate their content to inmates of varying cultures, and backgrounds. In contrast, engagement in learning is the visible outcome of motivation, and redirecting energy in the pursuit of a goal (Feistritzer & Haar, 2008). Teachers that do not understand culturally responsive teaching or have a lack of training in culturally responsive teaching may cause the students feelings of embarrassment (Feistritzer & Haar). Some people enjoy sharing personal information with others who are relatively unknown to them when teaching adults (Galbraith, 2004).

Statement of Purpose

The purpose of this project is to develop a handbook for the educational departments of correctional agencies in the process of in-service training for their teaching staff. The development of this project focuses on three main areas; incompatibilities in adult prison educational programs, culturally responsive teaching in adult prison educational programs, and learning theory in adult prison educational programs.

Methodology

The data for this study was collected and analyzed from adults currently in prison educational programs. Teachers rely on the correctional staff to guide them in styles of communication and methods for solving problems in their classroom (Cartledge, Gardner & Ford, 2009). Teachers must have a firm understanding of different cultures, gender gaps, and how different ethnic groups learn, will help the teacher become successful when they try new teaching strategies (Cartledge et al.).

Conclusions and Recommendations

Studies have shown that there is considerable need for education in adult prisons, and political bureaucracy is disabling prison educational programs by suffocating programs with economical demise (Campbell, 2005). Teachers become reluctant to pay the extra cost to learn andragogy teaching practices; therefore teachers are unprepared to deal with adult students that practice and demonstrate criminal behavior. Improving teachers' ability to teach is obviously crucial to school success, and that is the purpose of professional development (Dipaola & Hoy, 2006).

ACKNOWLEDGMENTS

The completion of this project would not have been possible without the help and professionalism of all those who contribute to this project. Thanks to Sam Williams his support in the effort to complete this project in time. Many hours were spent researching and debating the competencies known to be successful with developing a handbook that would best serve both the teachers and the correctional staff.

I am deeply grateful to the administrator at California Department of Corrections, for his unselfish efforts in helping to move the project forward and help to realize the vision for creating a model for classroom manage and leadership.

A special thanks to my coworkers for fully supporting this project since its inception. I thank them for proofreading my papers over and over, and for the many hours reviewing each phase of the project. I am also indebted to the teachers for allowing me to interview them during their lunch hour, and thanks to all of those who helped bring this document to fruition. A special thanks to my wife for her editorial support, sound suggestions, and attention to detail that helped to improve the final version of this project.

Chapter 1

INTRODUCTION

Background

The purpose of this project is to design a handbook that will help improve the teaching strategies of adult literacy prison educational programs that can be used as a reference manual. This correctional education research focuses on three areas:

1. Correctional Institutions
2. Teaching and Management Conditions
3. Culturally Responsive Teaching and Learning Theory

Correctional institutions and teaching and management conditions includes, but is not limited to, correctional officers, VS inmates, teacher VS inmates, and inmates versus peers. All of these elements play a critical role in the success or failure of the adult prison education program. Inmates do not go to prison to get an education, and correctional officers are reminded on a daily basis that criminals will respond with criminal behavior when they run out of options to resolve problems in a logical way. Correctional officers respond to fights, stabbing, suicide attempts, and verbal, as well as physical assaults. They are also trained to respond in aggressive ways towards inmates, providing more reasons why correction educational programs are failing (Campbell, 2005). Correctional officers provide their own form of disruptions in the prison regarding their educational programs. With mass handling of inmates, countless ways of humiliating inmates in order to make them subservient to rules, orders and special rules of behavior, are designed to maintain social distance between officers and inmates. Campbell (2005) claimed that frisking of inmates, regimented movement to work, eat, play, and drab prison clothing, all tend to depersonalize inmates. It also reinforces their belief that authority in the department of corrections is too opposed and not cooperative with correctional authorities. Therefore, how can educational programs function properly under these conditions? Correctional officers (CO's) assigned to educational programs should have special training in social-work and psychology as a component of the internal organization. Campbell (2005) stated internal collaboration encouraged employees to become more invested in the success of correctional educational programs, they have a better understanding of the programs goals, and it benefits both the correctional organization and the educational department. According to Muth, Gehring, Puffer, Mayers, Kamusikiri and Pressley (2009), too frequently, COs become so accustomed to responding to fights and operating in crisis mode, that they continue to function in that mode even when the situation does not demand it. Disrupting the learning process and many opportunities for useful collaboration between custody, staff and education staff are overlooked.

Positive attitudes toward prisoners are important in securing the effectiveness of various correctional rehabilitation programs and the successful reintegration of prisoners after release. Positive attitudes toward prisoners are important in securing the effectiveness of various correctional rehabilitation programs and the successful reintegration of prisoners after release. It is the responsibility of the prison warden and unit leaders to build trust, and to develop a commitment to the vision for the program. Without their support, the program is set up for failure. Making the vision clear is a process, and the goal cannot be accomplish with just one staff meeting. Part of the goal would have to be several meetings and in-service trainings, making sure that all staff had a clear understanding of what the vision and mission of the program (Kjelsberg, Skoglund & Rustad, 2007). An example of leadership can be set by modeling attitudes and behavior that support the vision, rewarding achievement of goals that support the vision. This strategy may not turn a lethargic bureaucracy into a cutting edge educational program, but it will carve a notch in the R of (CDCR) California Department of Corrections Rehabilitation and help redefine what it stands for (Campbell, 2005). Vision cannot be established in an organization, by edit, or by the exercise of power or coercion, but an act of persuasion, of creating an enthusiastic and dedicated commitment to a vision because it is right for the times, right for the organization, and right for the people who are working in it (Bennis & Banus, 2005).

In the correctional education department, teachers need to be aware that management conditions in the prison system do not begin and end with correctional officers. Teachers who contract with the prison system have duties that may cause incompatibilities within the educational department. To be effective, teachers in adult education need to know that adult learning is inextricably intertwined with adult development and adult learning will vary primary with stages of cognitive development (Knowles, Holton & Swanson, 2005). Understanding how to manage conditions in correctional education programs will help teachers understand that adult prison inmates have a host of unresolved personal issues. Once understood, it will allow teachers to examine their words or ideas carefully before challenging or commenting on student's classroom etiquette. Teachers who are not trained in methods of correctional teaching and management conditions in adult prison educational programs may not understand. According to Knowles et al. (2005), adult motivation to learn is the sum of four factors:

1. Success, adults want to be successful learners.
2. Volition, adults want to feel a sense of choice in their learning.
3. Value, adults want to learn something they value.
4. Enjoyment, adults want to experience the learning as pleasurable.

Teachers that lack an understanding of multicultural and prison politics will only cause confusion in the classroom. Joshee and Johnson (2007) suggested when teachers move towards a laissez-fair approach to teaching, rather than choose not to reeducate themselves to encourage equality and respect allows for better classroom management conditions. In educational programs, conditions that give uncertainty a chance to reveal its ugly head when multicultural educational strategies are not developed.

Feistritzer and Haar (2008) claimed that teachers who enter their profession though alternate routes, reflected a higher degree of mobility than did teachers in the overall teaching force. This allows many different life experiences that provide understanding as regards to empowering the inmate. Specifically, empowerment is not about making smart inmates smarter, or giving power to the inmate, but aiding them and teaching them to have the ability to think critically at a moment's notice.

Richards (2007) stated teaching and learning system cannot waive the teachers' contribution and the personal human contact between the student and teacher. Learning Theory of course is at the center of all educational programs. In regard to prison, it is a complex learning environment, problems in the classroom can often be the result of subject, and how the teacher presents the subject. This study was conducted at one of California's state prisons where subjects in prison curriculum dealt with race, racial power, and sexuality. Although there are more inmates of color in prisons, Europeans make up a majority of the teaching staff, which accounts for effects of culture on learning. In adult education the teacher is there to serve as a coach and resource, sharing in the learning process rather than controlling it. Teachers must keep in mind that prison programs are voluntarily, the fact that inmates come to the program is an indication that some inmates have a desire to learn. Inmates are unlikely to view literacy as something meaningful to their lives, especially the older ones who have survived without knowing how to read (Mayes, Cutri, Rogers & Montero, 2007). Learning theory confronts educational issues at both ends of the teaching and learning spectrum, and can make a class run smooth with the least classroom disruption (Mayes et al.). According to Powell and Caseau (2004), this partnership can be influenced by several factors sharing authority, and thus, reducing subjective differences between teachers and the students. Cowdery, Ingling-Rogers, Morrow and Wilson (2007) suggested the task for the teacher would be to establish an appropriate micro—cultural within the prison sub-cultural that will provide a relaxing climate and space to work in their racially segregated minds. In the realm of prison education, inmates stay within a comfort zone. Until a certain level of trust is established between the teacher and the inmate, learning progresses slowly and eventually comes to a halt.

Teachers can use the student's prior life experiences by adding positive rein-forcers while students recall their past. Teachers that use effective leadership skills can foster, develop and maintain relationships within diverse prison settings, and establish and accomplish effective goals with their students. Motivation is another area of student learning theory. Hoosain and Salili (2005) suggested that motivation takes into consideration the students' personal, socio-culture, and contextual factors. Factors such as meanings, goals, values, and perceptions of causes of success and failure in a specific situation are considered important determinants of achievement motivation. Therefore, teachers need to plan to create these conditions, because motivation resides inside all learners, children as well as adults. Cowdery et al. (2007) suggested that changing roles from givers of information, to facilitators and resource providers, is a difficult transition for many teachers. So it is best to begin where teachers feel most comfortable. Teachers need to plan to create these conditions because motivation resides inside all learners and children, as well as adults (Cowdery et al., 2007) stated teachers are in constant search of ways to help students develop the levels of competence and literacy needed in their research and study skills to move to a higher level of education.

Powell and Caseau (2004) stated that culture is learned. Shared values, beliefs, and behaviors are common to a particular group of people and individuals are taught, sometimes implicitly, sometimes explicitly, to view the world in a certain way and behave in ways that support this point of view. Some teachers are naïve to cultural individual identity and make the mistake of assuming all students learn the same by mainstream American standards only serve to reinforce the ideal of being viewed as inferior and their culture is not worth considering. Teachers must relate the content to the various cultural backgrounds of their learners. Teaching that ignores or trivializes adult learners' norms of behavior and communication provokes resistance that may elicit frustration. Joy or determination may differ across cultures, because cultures differ in their definitions of novelty, intimacy, opportunity, and gratification and in their definitions of appropriate responses (Barron et al., 2006). Whether identified as a 'color', as female, or 'male', or 'trans', 'lesbian' or straight or 'bisexual or 'queer', people have all been trained to evaluate ourselves and each other according to the existing labels (Wood et al., 2005). Teachers who know and understand that these conditions exist, acquire knowledge of the culture that will allow the teacher to clarify attitudes and values that includes recognizing, accepting, and celebrating diversity as a fundamental fact and salient part of human life (Joshee & Johnson, 2007).

Creating cultural pluralism in the classroom is no easy task, especially in prison (Bryson, 2005). Culturally responsive teaching efforts and cooperative learning that engage cultural diversity should be a common feature in andragogy practices that help implement multicultural practices to be developed appropriately for teachers, students, lesson plans and prison administrators. Teaching styles should be modified to allow variability, active participation, and novelty in learning. Multi-cultural education should be used as a yard stick to measure relevance, and effectiveness of teaching and communication styles (Campbell, 2005). The possibilities are unlimited in making education more effective for culturally diverse students.

Purpose of the Project

The purpose of this project is to design a handbook that will help improve the teaching strategies of teachers who work in adult prison educational programs. Before this project can begin in earnest, however, it is important to frame the issue. What are the outcomes and impact? Why is it important to examine them? The outcome for this project is to review the changes that take place in teachers as a result of their participation in the culturally responsive teaching project. The problem at the research site is the teachers are untrained in dealing with inmates in adult correctional educational programs. Teachers push their emergency alarm unnecessarily, thereby disrupting class activities and creating cognitive dissonance in the classroom. This is because teachers who are not trained in culturally responsive teaching, do not understand the dynamics of adult inmate students.

The adult correctional student often has been poor, unskilled, unemployed or underemployed. Teachers were observed during classroom interaction with students. One teacher in particular was very negative toward students not allowing other students to speak, or express themselves openly; at times arguing with students and distracting them from the learning process. This manual will help teachers new to correctional classroom experience and improve teachers' communication skills and help them understand the dynamics of prison educational programs. Often, offenders have a pervasive history of negative educational experiences, and teachers that are not trained in andragogy teaching methods will not have the skills to reduce the amount of frustration associated with classroom work that's all too common for the typical adult correctional student.

During the project classroom observation, it was observed that some of the teachers did not feel comfortable in their multicultural prison classroom. Correctional officers would disrupt the class, remove students and strip search them. The students would then return to class, causing cognitive dissonance in the classroom and learning would come to a halt. This manual is to give teachers tools to address disparities in the correctional classroom. The majority of prospective teachers in the California State Prison Educational Programs are white, while a majority of the students are minority. Meanwhile, the increase of minority inmates has caused a cultural mismatch in correctional education programs. This manual can be used as a guide for teachers, especially those who are not highly acculturated, to navigate the complex application and entry procedures that teaching programs typically require. There is also the challenge of teacher comfort, and feeling safe and welcome in a monoculture environment that is not their own.

Definition of Terms

Administrative Segregation (Ad-Seg): When a prisoner is being investigated and goes to the hole (Ad-Seg), until the investigation is complete. See Segregation.

Blocks: Cell houses.

Books: Administratively controlled account ledger which lists each prisoner's financial account balance of monies earned or sent to the inmate.

Care Package: Food or clothing sent from a friend or family member.
Contract: A written agreement between a prisoner and prison administration that allows a prisoner to be released from a Detention Unit with probation-like stipulations.

CUS: Custody Unit Supervisor/Cell-House supervisor.

Disciplinary Segregation (De-Seg): When a person is in the "hole" for an infraction.

Gate Time: At most jails/prisons (See Lock-up).

The Hole: An isolation (segregation) cell, used as punishment for the most paltry of offenses as well as serious offenses.

House: Cell.

Inmate: Considered a derogatory term by some prisoners (opposed to convict). Used by guards and administrators, or some inmates who are fish (first-timers and new arrivals who do not know the lingo).

Lock-Down: When prisoners are confined to their cells. Med-Line: Medication line, or pill-line.

Protective Custody (PC): Also as in "He's a PC case", meaning weak or untrustworthy.

Sallyport: Security area where guards enter the institution. Scan Call: Monitored telephone call. where prisoners are kept apart from the main population and denied most all privileges.

Shake-Down: Search.

Short: A prisoner who is close to his release date.

Slammed: "He's slammed down," meaning locked in the hole or Ad

Seg (Administrative Segregation)

State Issue: Any item that is provided by the state.

Store Commissary: Where a prisoner may purchase food, health, or

welfare items.

Tag/Write-Up: Infraction of institution rules.

Work-Line: When cells are opened so prisoners can report to work.

Yard-In: A command given to an inmate return to their cell; Closing

of the recreation yard.

Limitations

The purpose of this project is to design a handbook that will help improve the teaching strategies of adult prison educational programs, and can be used as a reference manual. Limitations in this project begin with the correction administrator. The California Department of Corrections (CDC) has procedures that are put in place to follow the chain of command. Approval for this project had to come from the prison administrator down to the prison coordinator. These procedures considerably slowed down the process. Other limitations included the lack of research in culturally responsive teaching in adult prison educational programs. Studies in culturally responsive teaching, learning theory, and culture theory were collected, compared and contrasted to create this paper.

Significance of the Project

The development and dissemination of high-quality, culturally responsive teaching materials are intended for widespread program improvement and replication. Culturally responsive teaching methods will be immediately helpful for teachers with less than two years teaching experiences. The culturally responsive teaching manual would provide a vehicle to engage in self-study and assist in the beginnings of change or in continuous program improvement. The program administrators are the gatekeepers for this process. They are the only ones who can decide if adopting these materials strengthens what teachers do, as they assist educational entities with excellence in education. The long-term benefits of the project are at least twofold. First, prison institutions that adopt project materials will broaden access to culture learning opportunities for students and increase student services for individuals with learning disabilities. Second, correctional institutions will be able to work as a team with teaching staff. This project offers an innovative solution to a widespread problem in the correctional education department that has potential for large-scale adoption and implementation. This will aid both correction staff and teaching staff within the institutions. It is expected that the prison educational program will adopt project materials during the school year and added to the education program. This project represents a major attempt to reform persistent problems in correctional education using known strategies of culturally responsive teaching, and learning theory in the correctional education system itself. The results will be immediately useable throughout the county, it is expected that adoption and implementation rates will be significant.

Organization of the Remainder of the Project

This material provides a quick over of the literature review, and will serve as an indicator for what will be discussed in Chapter 2. This section will give teachers a focal point, and prepare them for the reading in the following chapters.

Chapter 2

REVIEW OF THE RELATED LITERATURE

Introduction

The purpose of this project is to design a handbook that will help to improve the teaching strategies of adult prison educational programs that can be used as a reference manual. The conceptual framework of the project is based on the following literature: Management Conditions and Correctional Institutions Teaching; Culturally Responsive Teaching and Learning Theory.

Correctional Institutions Teaching
and Management Conditions

Correctional institutions teaching and management conditions includes, but is not limited to, correctional officers versus inmates, teacher versus inmates. It is when the inmate challenges the teachers' knowledge of prison procedures and the willingness of teachers to enforce prison policies. Inmates versus peers develop as classes are finished for that day. Often, inmates challenge their peers who conform to class regulations, by fighting with their peers, forcing them to act out in class (Travis, 2005). All of these elements play a critical role in the success or failure of the adult prison education program. Campbell (2005) found that inmates do not go to prison to get an education. Further, correctional officers are reminded on a daily basis that criminals will respond with criminal behavior when they run out of options to resolve problems in a logical way. Correctional officers respond to fights, stabbing, suicide attempts, and verbal as well as physical assaults and are trained to respond in aggressive ways towards inmates. All provide more reasons why correction educational programs are failing. It has long been acknowledged that criminal justice and corrections resemble the parable of the blind men who each touched a different part of an elephant and learned only from their narrow experience of what the elephant was like—the tail like a rope, the trunk like a snake, and the leg like a tree

(Campbell, 2005). This parable portrays a group of two or more people who have a significant mutual performance need or opportunity, but lack a focus on collective performance. Although teachers and correctional staff may refer to themselves as a team, their lack of collective focus and commitment will derail performance of the program.

Secondary education in prison came about as a result of public outcry. The public was tired of seeing their loved ones return home in worse mental condition than before they went to prison. Historically, correctional organizations have not engaged in correctional teaching and management conditions to provide collaborative efforts in educational, and social work programs in prisons (Muth et al., 2009). Inmates have significantly experienced more failure than success in their endeavors, and as a result, have learned to get attention and peer-group approval through misbehavior and eventually, anti-social acts (Muth et al.). Some inmates have failed marriages, child support issues, failed or dropped out of school, repeated felonies, as well as their own short—comings. This pattern of failure has prevented many inmates from having respect for themselves and others, creating more imaginary walls and obstacles to rehabilitation, including culturally responsive teaching and learning (Souryal, 2009).

Correctional officers provide their own form of disruptions in the prison in regards to educational programs. With mass handling of inmates, and countless ways of humiliating inmates in order to make them subservient to rules and orders, special rules of behavior are designed to maintain social distance between officers and inmates. Campbell (2005) claimed that frisking of inmates, regimented movement to work, eat, play, and drab prison clothing all tend to depersonalize inmates and reinforce their belief that authority in the department of corrections is too opposed, not cooperated with correctional authorities.

Therefore, how can correctional teaching and management conditions in educational programs function properly under these conditions? Correctional officers (CO's) assigned to educational programs should have special training in social-work, and psychology as a component of the internal organization. This will aid educational programs to take inmates who have failed throughout life, and help them develop adequate social and behavioral controls (Campbell, 2005). Creation of structure designed to ensure program integrity and effectiveness involves the formulation of written policies and procedures and the determination of who will be responsible for the operation of the programs. Campbell stated that internal collaboration encouraged employees to become more invested in the success of correctional educational programs, and they also have a better understanding of the programs goals, and benefits both the correctional organization and the educational department. According to Muth et al. (2009), too frequently, COs become so accustomed to responding to fights and operating in crisis mode that they continue to function in that mode even when the situation does not demand it, disrupting the learning process and many opportunities for useful collaboration between custody staff and education staff are overlooked. Leaders who take advantage of collaborative opportunities provide openings for employees to become more actively engaged in the organization. Positive attitudes toward prisoners are important in securing the effectiveness of various correctional rehabilitation programs and the successful reintegration of prisoners after release. CO's are in the positions of authority, and explicitly or implicitly, promise to frame their judgments and actions to match the standards of their profession or position according their oath (Kjelsberg, Hilding, Skoglund & Rustad, 2007).

It is the responsibility of the prison warden and unit leaders to build trust, and to develop a commitment to the vision for the program. Without their support, the program is setup for failure making the vision clear is a process, the goal cannot be accomplish with just one staff meeting. Part of the goal would be to have several meetings and in-service training making sure that all staff had a clear understanding of what the vision and mission of the program (Kjelsberg et al., 2007).

Campbell (2005) stated that the most powerful method for building commitment to the vision is for the executive and senior-level leaders to model that commitment. Employees look to leaders for direction and guidance. If leaders' actions demonstrate their commitment to the vision, employees will follow out of respect for both the positional authority and the personal power of the leadership group. An example of leadership can be set by modeling attitudes and behavior that support the vision, rewarding achievement of goals that support the vision. This strategy may not turn a lethargic bureaucracy into a cutting edge educational program, but it will carve a notch in the R of (CDCR) and help redefine what it stands for (Campbell, 2005). Vision cannot be established in an organization, by edit, or by the exercise of power or coercion, but an act of persuasion, of creating an enthusiastic and dedicated commitment to a vision because it is right for the times, right for the organization, and right for the people who are working in the program (Moore, 2005).

Campbell (2005) suggested that the correctional environment can be dangerous for offenders who are especially vulnerable to the abuse of power by correctional personnel, as well as predatory attacks by other offenders. It is also dangerous for correctional personnel, who must maintain order and defend themselves and others against the potential of violence by inmates, to remain within the bounds of the law and codes of conduct. Abuse of power is a constant fear for both offenders and correctional staff and continues to create problems in correctional teaching and management conditions. Campbell (2005) suggested ethical behavior begins with good management leadership set by clear goals and objectives that provide an effective organizational structure that clearly ensures the alignment and/or defines lines of authority, responsibility, and communication. Development of the organizational and administrative systems, to ensure the development of policies, practices, and procedures support the correctional agency vision that result in an organization. Structure that promotes the organization's mission, evaluate coordination, cooperation, and integration between divisions progress toward desired outcomes of correctional teaching and management conditions.

Campbell (2005) stated demographic differences among staff and offenders—ethnicity, race, religion, gender, age, and nationality—may also influence correctional teaching and management conditions. Such differences may affect how people view power: for some, it has a negative connotation; others expect people in positions of authority to exercise power. Because the demographic makeup of staff and offenders is likely to vary in different parts of the United States, the geographic location of a correctional agency/organization may also influence its culture, along with the leadership of the correctional agency/ organization can also affect its culture. For example, if the leadership values diversity, the correctional agency/organization may have more women and people of color in management positions, which can affect the social architecture. Correctional staff who are newly arrived from other countries or are first-generation Americans may view power and its appropriate use through a different cultural lens. The multiple groups that make up the social architecture of an organization and the different perspectives these groups represent, influence how power is viewed in the organization.

To use power effectively, a leader must be aware this condition exists (Campbell, 2005).

Inmates base their whole existence on respect; this is where effective personnel management strategies can help the teachers and correctional staff to demonstrate values, ethics based on respect, competence, and accountability (Campbell, 2005). In the correctional education department, teachers need to be aware that management conditions in the prison system do not begin and end with correctional officers. Teachers who contract with the correctional department have duties that may cause management problems within the educational department that include report writing that may result in a student being removed from the educational program. Teachers in adult education need to know that adult learning is inextricably intertwined with adult development and adult learning will vary with stages of cognitive development (Knowles et al., 2005).

Failure to remove inmates from programs gives them a false sense of power; therefore teachers must be resilient and find other methods of classroom management that stay within the boundaries of CDCR rules and regulations (Keating, 2007). There is a need to identify which correctional teaching and management methods work with specific types of offenders, and then determine if the methods can be replicated for inmates that come to class with a different set of values, defined by lifelong experiences, and rules created by a prison sub-culture (Campbell, 2005).

Understanding how to manage conditions in correctional education programs will help teachers understand that adult prison inmates have a host of unresolved personal issues, allowing teachers to examine their words or ideas carefully before challenging or commenting on student's classroom etiquette. Keating (2007) stated that framing each course how material is presented begins with the syllabus and includes course objectives, teaching objectives and self definition. Teaching adult inmates can be both energizing and self actualizing, or exhausting and frustrating. What determines the end result will be the teacher's ability to effectively deliver their lesson through effective instruction facilitation.

Gay (2000) stated that academic demands are complemented with the emotional support and facilitative instruction; a coaching style rather than a dictatorial style of teaching should be used and reciprocal responsibility for learning is developed. Gay (2000) suggested that disparities in classroom interactional opportunities are affected by many different variables, most of which have little to do with the intellectual abilities of students.

Muffoletto and Horton (2007) suggested learning that is related to the student or individual as a group member should be included. empirical knowledge. A category of comparative ethics, aesthetics, or ethnology; Cultural diversity is recognition of pre-given cultural "contents" and customs, held in a time frame of relativism. Cultural diversity is also the representation of a radical rhetoric of the separation of totalized cultures, safe in the Utopianism of a mythic memory of as unique collective identity.

Enrichment of understanding of the world and his place in it can be enhanced by helping the student relate to his cultural heritage as well as to understand his potential place in modern society. Campbell (2005) claimed the worldview is composed of all things people have learned, all of our experiences. Correctional teaching and management conditions define and direct the ways in which teachers interpret this information and thus, how students react to new information in traditional schools, as well as in prison educational programs. European Americans defined life by the preponderance of middle-class values, beliefs and attitudes. American classrooms are moving towards a more multicultural holistic setting, with transformation ideals. Keating (2007) claimed the transformational multiculturalism holistic, connectionist approach, leads to new forms of individual and collective agency that makes change possible, although not inevitable. Transformation has to go through the body, through the physical, the emotional, and the spiritual. Once transformation has enacted it disrupts and changes everything from family life to relationships with others on every level, such as social, job, leisure, etc. (Bartolome, 2008). Today, prisons are dominated by the minority populations, and a majority of the teachers are European

Americans (Whites). According to Campbell (2005), prisons do not go out of the way to insure that teachers are trained to understand cultural responsive teaching that includes learning theories, or management conditions in the correctional classroom. For democracy in the classroom to be successful, prisons need to consider training for teachers that stimulates them, and teaches them not to focus only on beliefs and value systems. Teachers should also be aware of how their own cultural values and attitudes affect their teaching strategies and the harmony in their classroom (Sandlin & Walther, 2009).

Teachers who are not trained in methods of correctional teaching and management conditions in adult prison educational programs may not understand that adult motivation to learn is the sum of four factors:

1. Success, adults want to be successful learners.

2. Volition, adults want to feel a sense of choice in their learning.

3. Value, adults want to learn something they value.

4. Enjoyment, adults want to experience the learning as pleasurable (Knowles et al., 2005, p. 109).management conditions in prison educational programs will only cause confusion in the classroom; prison education programs are, in many respects, coalitions of interest groups. To successfully influence inmates (students) requires understanding of who has power in the organization and how to access it (Sandlin &

Walther, 2009). The two most important steps for leaders who want to exercise influence with students are to know their own agenda and to understand the environment in which they want to implement that agenda. They can use a variety of tactics to accomplish these steps. After setting the agenda and mapping the political terrain, they need to select the implementation tactics that are most likely to achieve the influence they envision (Sandlin & Walther).

When teachers move towards a laissez-fair approach, rather than choose not to reeducate themselves, they are rejecting equality and respect that allows for better classroom management conditions in educational programs. Those conditions allow uncertainty a chance to reveal its ugly head when multicultural educational strategies are not developed (Joshee & Johnson, 2007). The notion of correctional institutions teaching and management conditions has received much attention in recent years, though much of this has tended to focus more on public schools rather than prison education programs (Bjork, Johnston & Ross, 2007). Some authors linked this lesser focus on effective correctional institutions teaching and management conditions to the absence of agreement on what this notion actually represents in a sector that lacks a unified view of its purpose (Joshee & Johnson, 2007).

There are strong links between prison environment and the success or failure of prison education programs. These dimensions of prison environment are physical and psychological including respect and freedom or lack of it, and all inmates will come to terms with their existence behind the prison walls. On the other hand, teachers could make the difference and the education department could offer them a chance to get off the repetitive cycle of incarceration and overcome some of the psychological influences and effects of the institution (Mayes et al., 2007). Teachers who choose to work in adult prison educational programs should have global knowledge when dealing with inmates. Global knowledge enriches their understanding of domestic educational policy debates and the concrete realities of local prison systems. Further, teacher education in an increasingly interconnected world requires enhanced content knowledge, fresh approaches to teaching, and explicit acknowledgement within teacher education programs. Local, national and global educational discourses and practices directly affect the professional responsibilities of American teachers (Bjork et al., 2007).

Feistritzer and Haar (2008) claimed that teachers who enter teaching though alternate routes also reflected a higher degree of mobility than different life experiences, therefore; allowing them understanding that empowering the inmate is not about making smart inmates smarter, and not about giving power to the inmate, but aiding them and teaching them to have the ability to think critically at a moment's notice.

Culturally Responsive Teaching

Ryndak (2006) found teaching adults encourages knowledge construction by experiences with complex real-life problems. Adult students take responsibility for their own learning as they identify what they already know from life experiences helps them to work independently as they research different aspects of their life before bringing their findings back and present them to the class. The teacher's main role in adult teaching is to facilitate while allowing students to use their experience to resolve learning issues. Knowles et al. (2005) stated self-directness has perhaps been the most debated aspect of andragogy and it is also important to consider that understanding effectiveness in culturally responsive teaching varies in relation to the students' conception of learning and teaching. Kember and Gow (1994) claimed learning is seen as a reproductive process, fostering a preference for didactic teaching; one where learning is conceived of in constructivist terms, by 'self-determining' students encouraging learners to favor a more facilitative approach. Gay (2000) suggested if teachers are to carry out effective culturally responsive teaching, they need to understand how ethnically diverse students learn. It is necessary because the processes of learning, not the intellectual capability, used by students from different ethnic groups, are influenced by their cultural socialization (Stengel & Tom, 2006).

Powell and Caseau (2004) stated that culture is learned and shared values, beliefs, and behaviors are common to a particular group of people. Also, individuals are taught, sometimes implicitly, sometimes explicitly, to view the world in a certain way and behave in ways that support this point of view. Effective teachers in adult prison education, who understand culture in relation to intrinsic value in adult education, adopt culturally and linguistically meaningful teaching strategies (Barron, Grimm & Gruber, 2006). The complementary approaches of critical ethnography and learning theories that recognize the importance of a student's home, community, and culture is considered a valuable tool in lieu of rigid models based on social stereotypes or social stratification.

Teachers must have a clear understanding of the instructional requirements for empowering all students in adult correctional classrooms, especially those who are different culturally, socially, racially, or economically. Teachers must relate the content to the various cultural backgrounds of their learners. Teaching that ignores or trivializes adult learners' norms of behavior and communication, provokes resistance that may elicit frustration, or determination may differ across cultures, because cultures differ in their definitions of novelty, intimacy, opportunity, and gratification and in their definitions of appropriate responses (Barron et al., 2006).

Behind the image of a model minority, there is the notion that good minorities are supposed to be grateful for having been accepted by the dominant White culture, while feeling content to stay one level below Whites because they can never fully measure up to their standards (Li & Beckett, 2006). Keating (2007) stated that reading whiteness and un-reading race describes and attempts to address some of the difficulties that can occur when educators incorporate analyses of whiteness into classroom instruction. When students who self-identify or are labeled as white are introduced to recent investigations of whiteness, they are forced to recognize the insidious roles whiteness plays in US culture. This recognition can trigger a variety of unwelcome reactions-ranging from guilt, withdrawal and despair, to anger and the construction of an extremely celebratory radicalized whiteness (Keating, 2007).

Keating (2007) stated although whiteness is one of the most difficult topics to include in classroom instruction, it is crucial that educators explore it in teaching. Teachers cannot analyze culturally specific dimensions of text by writers of colors without also examining 'whiteness, to do so further normalizes whiteness and thus reinforces the long standing hidden belief in 'white' invisibility as well as the white supremacist embedded within US culture.

Black cultural patterns have their roots in West Africa and are based on strong religious African culture marked by a distinct pattern of thinking, feeling and acting that has developed as a way of adapting to color discrimination. African Americans process information from the environment differently from other groups, they view things in their entirety and not as isolated parts (Proefriedt, 2008). According to Keating (2007), African Americans are not voluntary minorities, they are the only minorities enslaved in America. Therefore they do not subscribe to white class values, and these attitudes may affect how students respond to teachers from different cultures, and the information that is being taught. Asian Americans are another minority group that represents the prison makeup. Weis and Fine (2005) suggested that according to the 1990 US Census, there are about 7.3 million Asian Americans in this country. Asian Americans represent a very heterogeneous population whose members practice various ranges of religious and philosophical orientations. The prisons are beginning to see as many as three percent of the Asian population behind prison walls (Weis & Fine, 2005). Weis and Fine suggested this gives reason why educators need to learn different cultural customs and communication styles that will serve to help teachers effectively, and to teach and communicate with members from different cultures. Weis and Fine stated that the widely observed silence of many Asian students who grow up in America is a problem for educators who draw on their own implicit models of intelligence and education. Teachers urge these students to participate more, to contribute more, and to talk more. Weis and Fine stated that while straight talking is a good way to convey one's meaning in Western contexts, it is indirectness that is a powerful theme of the East Asian's life. When silence is appreciated and valued with this perspective on talking, other forms of communication become important. The Japanese term 'ishin denshin', exemplifies this meaning-the communication between two minds that do not need words.

Hispanic Americans are the second largest inmate population in prison. Wood, Russell, Wilson and Ireton (2005) suggested that cultural understanding of the development of motivation is an essential backdrop for teaching Hispanic Americans. Motivation among Hispanics is shaped by cultural values, traditions, and expectations. For example, Hispanic students are more likely to attend to the needs of sick family member instead of attending class. When the student does not connect with the teacher, he or she is likely to focus on the family members instead of attending class (Wood et al., 2005). Thus, to understand Hispanic motivation, the culture needs to be taken into consideration in order to maintain a relevant worldview perspective.

Whether identified as color, as female or male, or as lesbian or straight, or bisexual or queer. Humans have all been trained to evaluate ourselves and each other according to the existing labels (Wood et al., 2005). Teachers who know and understand that these conditions exist, acquire knowledge of the culture that will allow the teacher to clarify attitudes and values that includes recognizing, accepting, and celebrating diversity as a fundamental fact and salient part of human life (Joshee & Johnson, 2007).

Powell and Caseau (2004) stated that a communication context has physical, social, and psychological features that include high context messages on one end and low context messages on the other. A high context message has most of the relevant information in the physical setting or is internalized within the person. Most of the meaning in the message is implied. Japanese, Hmong, Koreans, Chinese, and Latinos are examples of high context communities. Powell and Caseau (2004) further stated that low context groups require that the message includes a great deal of explicit information. Understanding different cultures in the classroom will bring the class closer towards pluralism in the classroom when working inside a correctional educational program.

Creating cultural pluralism in the classroom is no easy task, especially in prison (Bryson, 2005). Culturally responsive teaching efforts and cooperative learning that engages cultural diversity should be a common feature in andragogy practices. Efforts to implement multicultural practices should be developed appropriately for teachers, students, lesson plans and prison administrators. Teaching styles should be modified to allow variability, active participation, and novelty in learning to allow multi-cultural education to be used as a yard stick to measure relevance, and effectiveness of teaching and communication styles (Campbell, 2005).

The possibilities are unlimited in making education more effective for culturally diverse students with strategies designed to increase cognitive sophistication or complexity have been shown to have a positive impact on prejudice reduction (Cushner, McClelland & Safford, 2006). Cognitive complexity refers to the degree to which an individual differentiates, or makes distinctions between discrete aspects of an event, and/or makes connections or relationships among these elements. A person high in cognitive complexity is able to analyze or differentiate a situation into many constituent elements, and then explore connections and potential relationships among those elements.

Culturally responsive teaching strategies are designed to help individuals avoid stereotypes and over generalizations. They become aware of the biases in their thinking and behavior, which helps them become less prejudiced (Cushner et al., 2006). According to Sleeter and Grant (2003), educators are cautioned against assuming that students from low-status groups develop poor self-concepts at home, especially if they are not behaving as the teacher expects. According to Sleeter and Grant, often the assumptions of these educators are not true. For example, considerable research has been done on various dimensions of the self—concepts and self-esteem of African American and White American student (Sleeter & Grant). A review of this research repeatedly found that young African Americans express above-average levels of self-esteem; often more so than those of White students of the same age. Knowing the social hostility their children will have to face, many African American parents and other parents of color deliberately build up their children's sense of belonging to a strong group, so that they enter school feeling good about themselves, their personal abilities, and their racial or ethnic group (Sleeter & Grant).

According to Diller and Moule (2005), educators differ somewhat about the role of schools in bringing about change in the lives of students and exactly where the change process should be located. Is it better to change students to fit their circumstances in the greater society, or to educate students to try to change the world around them? These are technically referred to as autoplactic and alloplactic solutions. Helping individuals cope with difficult life situations by accommodating or adapting to them (changing the person) is autoplastic; encouraging or teaching individuals to impose changes on the external environment so that it better fits their needs is alloplactic. According to Diller and Moule (2005), cultures of color differ widely on this issue. Asian American culture, for example, tends to stress passive acceptance of reality and transcendence of conflict by adjusting perceptions so that harmony can be achieved with their environment. African Americans, on the other hand, tend to point to a racist environment as the cause of many of their distresses and advocate changing it rather than changing themselves. Northern European culture, for its part, tends to encourage the confrontation of obstacles in the environment that restrict freedom, but this is not necessarily the position taken by most white teachers. Diller and Moule suggested that much student behavior can be understood as a result of their beliefs about locus of control and locus of responsibility. Locus of control refers to whether individuals feel that they are in control of their own fate (internal control) or are being controlled externally (external control) and have little impact on the outside world. Locus of responsibility refers to whether individuals believe they are responsible for their own fate (internal responsibilities) or cannot be held responsible because more powerful forces are at work (external responsibility). Generally, European American teachers believe in internal control and internal responsibility and individuals are in control of their own fate, their actions affect outcomes, and success or failure in life is related to personal characteristics and abilities. Because of the absoluteness with which the student experiences socialization, he or she begins, early on, to share the human tendency to view the world from his or her own perspective and begin to believe that his or her way is certainly the best way. According to Cushner et al. (2006), this perspective is called ethnocentrism, which refers to the tendency people have to evaluate others according to their own standards and is an almost universal result of socialization. One major expression of ethnocentrism is a strong resistance to change. Cushner et al. clearly stated that ethnocentrism alone is not sufficient. Researchers also need to make sense out of the busy world, and to do so, they use schemata. Another term for such schemata is category. Categorization is the cognitive process through which human beings simplify their world by putting similar stimuli into the same group. The kind of categories that are used, how narrow or broad they are, and what meaning are attached to them, are all shaped by culture and acquired through socialization (Cushner et al.).

Cushner et al. (2006) suggested stereotypes are examples of categories of people. Research found that the process of categorization, along with ethnocentrism, combines to create a potentially harmful situation. Although any cultural group may teach its members to categorize other groups either positively or negatively, most stereotypes end up as negative labels placed on individuals because they are members of a particular group (Cushner et al., 2006).

According to Diller and Moule (2005), the critical factor in cross-cultural psychology is a fundamentally different way of being in the world. In no way does Western thinking address any system of cognition other than its own. Given that Judeo-Christian belief systems include notions of the creator putting human beings in charge of all creations, it is easy to understand why this group of people assumes that it also possesses the ultimate way of describing psychological phenomena for all of humanity. In reality, the thought that what is right comes from one worldview produces a narcissistic worldview that desecrates and destroys much of what is known as culture and cosmological perspective.

Knowles et al. (2005) stated culturally responsive teaching corrects many flaws in the deficiency orientation. It focuses on strengths, recognizes the legitimacy of various cultural experiences and routes to becoming a mature person, and does not advocate that a person be ashamed of or give up anything he or she is.

Culturally responsive teaching is liberating, it guides students in understanding that no single version of truth is total and permanent. It does not solely prescribe to mainstream ways of knowing. In order to accomplish this, teachers make authentic knowledge about different ethnic groups accessible to students. Gay (2000) stated the validation, information, and pride it generates are both psychologically and intellectually liberating. This freedom results in improved achievement of many kinds, including increased concentration on academic learning tasks. Gay stated other improved achievements can include clear and insightful thinking, more caring, concerned, and humane interpersonal skills, better understanding of interconnections among individual; local, national, ethnic, global, and human identities, and acceptance of knowledge as something to be continuously shared, critiqued, revised, and renewed.

Weis, McCarthy and Dimitradis (2006) stated teaching in prison posed a series of unique challenges. Prison culture and academic culture are, in a way, diametrically opposed and are closed institutions in which control is the primary concern and questioning authority is not tolerated. In academia, college and universities are highly open places that encourage questioning. According to Feistritzer and Haar (2008), operating a college inside a tightly closed institution where cerebral security always has primacy, requires adaptation, but the rewards that come from teaching an engaged group of students. The benefits to prisoners and society as a whole make the limitations, both structural and financial, worth enduring.

Teachers must relate the content to the various cultural backgrounds of their learners (Justice, 2006). Teachers who know and understand that these conditions exist acquire knowledge of the culture that will allow the teacher to clarify attitudes and values that include recognizing, accepting, and celebrating diversity as a fundamental fact and salient part of human life (Wesley, Rosenfeld & Siins-Gunzenhauser, 1993).

Spronken-Smith (2005) found teaching that ignores or trivializes adult learners' norms of behavior and communication provokes resistance and may elicit frustration, because cultures differ in their definitions of novelty, intimacy, opportunity, and gratification in their definitions of appropriate responses.

Learning Theory

Richards (2007) stated the teaching and learning system cannot waive the teachers' contribution and the personal human contact between the student and teacher. A change in the field of learning systems must take into account, data that belongs to the field of education and learning. Data including attitudes and the teachers' and students, ability and personality, psychological and sociological processes that accompany a process of change, the teaching method, the learning goals as well as cost versus effectiveness (Muffoletto & Horton, 2007). Learning Theory is at the center of all educational programs. In regard to prisons, it is a complex learning environment. Problems in the classroom can often be the result of the subject, and how the teacher presents the subject. This study was conducted at one of California's state prisons where subjects in prison curriculum dealt with race, racial power, and sexuality. Although there are more inmates of color in prisons, Europeans make up a majority of the teaching staff, which accounts for effects of culture on learning. Mayes et al. (2007) suggested students like to see representation of themselves standing in front of the classroom. Having a multicultural staff act as a reinforcement to help students identify with the material that is being presented. As a concept of secondary reinforcers, multicultural staffing is an important element in accounting for human learning. Traditionally, students are preconditioned to seeing a person of European descent in front of the classroom. Teachers and inmates should have educational experiences from various cultural perspectives, not from one point of view, with an example of leadership, and inter-subjectivity among themselves (Mayes et al., 2007).

In adult education, the teacher is there to serve as a coach and resource, sharing in the learning process rather than controlling it. Teachers must keep in mind that prison programs are voluntary, and the fact that inmates come to the program is an indication that some inmates have a desire to learn. Inmates are unlikely to view literacy as something meaningful to their lives, especially the older ones who have survived without knowing how to read (Mayes et al., 2007). Most of the inmates probably had little or any, formal education, thus they will be uncertain about their ability to learn, think and process information according to classroom standards. Learning theory confronts educational issues at both ends of the teaching and learning spectrum, and can make a class run smooth with the least classroom disruption (Mayes et al.). This partnership can be influenced by several factors sharing authority, and thus, reducing subjective differences between teachers and the students (Powell & Caseau, 2004). Cowdery et al. (2007) suggested the task for the teacher would be to establish an appropriate micro-cultural within the prison sub-cultural that will provide a relaxing climate and space to work in their racially segregated minds. Thomas and Thomas (2008) clearly suggested there is no single formula for conducting a class successfully, because the task is influenced by multiple conditions that vary from one place and time to another. Those conditions include the number of students in the class and their characteristics; the instructor's traits, the nature of the learning tasks the students face, the available teaching facilities, the schools policies, and more (Thomas & Thomas). In the realm of prison education, inmates stay within a comfort zone. Until a certain level of trust is established between the teacher and the inmate, learning progress slowly comes to a halt. Knowles et al. (2005) stated the core premise of learning style is that individual learner preferences will lead to learners being less effective in learning situations that require them to leave the comfort of their preferred learning strategies and styles. That is, people can learn how to learn differently from ways they naturally prefer.

Finally, Suskie and Banta (2009) stated as teachers understand how people learn, they are realizing that much of what students memorize is committed to short term memory and quickly forgotten. Because of these factors, educators are increasingly emphasizing thinking and other skills more so than knowledge and simple understanding. Knowledge and understanding are important outcomes of many courses and programs, but today they are less important than they were a generation or two ago (Suskie & Banta). In adult prisons, students learn and apply long term memory through prior life experience (Presseisen, 2008). Teachers can use the student's prior life experiences by adding positive rein-forcers while students recall their pass. Teachers who use effective leadership skills, foster, develop and maintain relationships within diverse prison settings, and establish and accomplish effective goals with their students. Presseisen (2008) stated adults are self direct learners who assess their needs and apply appropriate methods to learn to identify concepts that they can use for effective goal setting. They also create a positive vision for themselves and their future in order to set and reach obtainable goals.

Motivation

Motivation is an area of student learning theory. Hoosain and Salili (2005) suggested that motivation takes into consideration both personal, socio-culture, and contextual factors. Factors such as meanings, goals, values, and perceptions of causes of success and failure in a specific situation are considered important determinants of achievement motivation.

Donavant (2008) maintained that adults are intrinsically motivated towards learning, but that motivation is premised on their perception of the need to learn given material in relationship to their adult roles. Learning that is imposed on adults will be met with resentment and is minimally effective.

It is the responsibility of adult educators to accurately assess educational needs, including learners' willingness to participate in educational endeavors and their likelihood of success in those endeavors. Donavant (2008) suggested learning theory in culturally responsive teaching creates a learning atmosphere in which learners and instructors feel respected through the learned experience including learners' perspectives, and values. Knowles et al. (2005) suggested these conditions are essential for developing intrinsic motivation among students. Teachers need to plan to create these conditions, because motivation resides inside all learners, children as well as adults (Cowdery et al., 2007).

Learning theory helps the teacher break down stereotypes, and improve the identification of self in the realm of another person's world. Gay (2000) stated one premise of learning theory is that teaching and learning are cultural processes that make teaching and learning more accessible and equitable for a wide variety of students. The students' cultures need to be more clearly understood in a way that can be achieved by analyzing education from multiple cultural perspectives, and thereby removing the blindness imposed on education by the dominant cultural experience (Peters-Davis & Shultz, 2005). Admittedly, andragogy is not a panacea for adult education practices, but its usefulness as a rubric for better understanding for the adult learner should not be ignored.

Spronken-Smith (2005) suggested changing roles from givers of information to facilitators and resource providers is a difficult transition for many teachers, so begin where teachers feel most comfortable. During the project observation, there were two main discussions about facilitating groups. First was the power to control learning activities, and second, when and how to make interventions. The fundamental difficulty appeared to be that teachers were not sure of what they were trying to achieve in terms of student interaction. This was complicated by the need to work as members of a team.

During the implementation stage, the key concern for class participation was coming to terms with having less control over student-learning activities and content knowledge. The two less experienced teachers managed their groups much more closely than others. One of the teachers even set the agenda for each student meeting and both tended to direct the group rather than take a 'back seat' role preferred by some of the more experienced teachers.

Learning Theory can be applied in all educational programs and in regard to prison, complex learning environment problems in the classroom can often be the result of subject, and how the teacher presents the subject. The task then, is for the teacher to establish an appropriate micro-culture within the prison sub-culture that will provide a relaxing climate and space to work in their culturally segregated minds. Therefore, it is important teachers should begin their lesson where they are most comfortable, but teachers should remember to include learner's perspectives and values (Spronken-Smith, 2005). Knowles et al. (2005) suggested these conditions are essential for developing intrinsic motivation among students. Teachers need to plan to create these conditions, because motivation resides inside all learners, children as well as adults (Cowdery et al., 2007). Gillett and Hammond (2009) stated teachers are in constant search of ways to help students develop the levels of competence and literacy needed in their research and study skills to move to a higher level of education.

In learning theory, the teaching and learning system cannot waive the teachers' contribution, and the personal human contact between the student and teacher. A change in the field of learning systems must take many data that belong to the field of education and learning into account, including attitudes and the teachers' and students, learning theory helps the teacher break down stereotypes, and improve the identification of self in the realm of another person's world. Gay (2000) stated that one premise of learning theory is teaching and learning are cultural processes that make teaching and learning more accessible and equitable for a wide variety of students ability and personality, psychological and sociological process that accompany a process of change, the teaching method, the learning goals as well as cost versus effectiveness (Muffoletto & Horton, 2007). work has pulled together and integrated the knowledge base of theory and research that does exist on several culture-specific learning styles. This literature remains largely scattered throughout the journals of several disciplines although some single works in recent years have organized the learning style information on several groups better than others. Although no single existing book would serve as a comprehensive learning style textbook for use in teacher education programs, the use of two or three different books along with selected journal articles would provide sufficient coverage of the current state of cultural learning styles theory and research to improve considerably the cultural responsiveness of most teacher education programs (Smith).

Educators must remember that learning occurs within each individual as a continual process throughout life giving reasons why people learn at different speeds, so it is natural for students to be anxious or nervous when faced with a learning situation. Positive reinforcement by the instructor can enhance learning, as can proper timing of the instruction (Lieb, 1991).

According to Muffoletto and Horton (2007), learning results from stimulation of the senses. In some people, one sense is used more than others to learn or recall information this why instructors should present materials that stimulates as many senses as possible in order to increase their chances of teaching success.

There are four critical elements of learning that must be addressed to ensure that participants learn. These elements include motivation, reinforcement, retention and transference.

Lieb (1991) stated that if the participant does not recognize the need for the information (or has been offended or intimidated), all of the instructor's effort to assist the participant to learn will be in vain. The instructor must establish rapport with participants and prepare them for learning; this provides motivation. Instructors can motivate students via several means by setting a feeling or tone for the lesson. According to Lieb (1991), instructors should try to establish a friendly, open atmosphere that shows the participants they will help them learn. Set an appropriate level of concern. The level of tension must be adjusted to meet the level of importance of the objective. If the material has a high level of importance, a higher level of tension/stress should be established in the class. Lieb (1991) stated however, people learn best under low to moderate stress. If the stress is too high it becomes a barrier to learning. Set an appropriate level of difficulty. The degree of difficulty should be set high enough to challenge participants but not so high that they become frustrated by information overload. The instruction should predict and reward participation, culminating in success.

According to Lieb (1991), reinforcement is a very necessary part of the teaching/learning process; through it, instructors encourage correct used by instructors who are teaching participants new skills. As the name implies, positive reinforcement is 'good' and reinforces 'good' (or positive) behavior. According to Lieb (1991), negative reinforcement is the contingent removal of a noxious stimulus that tends to increase the behavior, the contingent presentation of a noxious stimulus that tends to decrease a behavior is called punishment. Reinforcing a behavior will never lead to extinction of that behavior by definition. Punishment and Time Out lead to extinction of a particular behavior, but positive or negative reinforcement of that behavior never will. When instructors are trying to change behaviors (old practices) they should apply both positive and negative reinforcement.

Lieb (1991) stated retention by the participants is directly affected by the amount of practice during the learning process while the instructors emphasize retention and application. After the students demonstrate correct (desired) performance, they should be urged to practice to maintain the desired performance. Distributed practice is similar in effect to intermittent reinforcement.

Transfer of learning is the result of training. It is the ability to use the information taught in the course but in a new setting. As with reinforcement, there are two types of transfer, positive and negative. According to Lieb (1991), positive transference, like positive reinforcement, occurs when the participants use the behavior taught in the course. Negative transference, again like negative reinforcement, occurs when the participants do not do what they are told. This results in a positive (desired) outcome.

Although adult learning theory is relatively new as field of study, it is just as substantial as traditional education and carries potential for greater success. Additionally, the learners come to the course with precisely defined expectations. Unfortunately, there are barriers to their learning. The best motivators for adult learners are interest and selfish benefit, if they can be shown that the course benefits them pragmatically, they will perform better, and the benefits will be longer lasting (Lieb, 1991).

Rationale

The purpose for this project was to study instructional practices useful in improving the teaching strategies of all teachers, strategies that can be used to manage conditions in correctional classrooms, improve understanding of different generations, and how students of different cultural backgrounds learn. Particularly, teachers working in a correctional education program with less than two years teaching experience. This suggests institutional and programmatic practices that will prepare future teachers for teaching in correctional education programs. The project's conceptual framework was informed by the literature reviewed in this chapter. Two areas of particular significance are learning theory and culturally responsive teaching. Cultural diversity poses an andragogical and social challenge to inexperienced educators working in the correctional system for the first time. Teaching effectively in culturally diverse classrooms means, using culturally sensitive strategies and content to ensure equitable opportunities for academic success. Culture can influence not only values, beliefs, and social interactions, but also how educators view the world, what educators consider important, what people attend to, and how people learn and interpret information.

Summary

Teaching and management practices included understanding where students come from, the need to watch very closely and listen very closely before one attacks. Teaching and management practices in adult prison educational programs require that teachers demonstrate both aesthetic caring and authentic caring in their classroom while also paying attention to the community context in which education takes place (Benham, 2005). With mass handing of inmates, countless ways of humiliating inmates in order to make them subservient to rules and orders, and drab prison clothing, all tend to depersonalize inmates and reinforce their belief that authority in the department of corrections is too opposed, not cooperated with correctional authorities (Campbell, 2005). It is the responsibility of the prison warden to build trust. Without this support, the program is set up for failure, and the goal cannot be accomplished. Creation of structure designed to ensure program integrity and effectiveness involves the formulation of written policies and procedures and is the only way teaching and management practices will survive in prison educational programs.

When using culturally responsive teaching methods, the possibilities are unlimited. Teaching strategies designed to increase cognitive sophistication or complexity can be used within multicultural prison educational classrooms when inmates (students) challenge teachers and teachers lack cultural competence and training to effectively manage correctional classrooms (Cushner et al., 2006). Diller and Moule (2005) suggested that teaching is good teaching, and good teaching in correctional classrooms requires the teacher to know the inner-workings of the correctional education programs, and the difficulties they will encounter while working in prison educational programs. Teaching is a talent but teachers must master the inner-workings of prisons. For example, when inmates are harassed by correctional officers and then return to class upset. Dealing with this type of distraction takes more than talent. Knowledge of how to deal with difficult inmates requires that teachers know culturally responsive teaching methods. Diller and Moule (2005) found that this knowledge will give teachers a platform or base of knowledge to begin with when inmates are often frustrated and unreachable. Inmates have significantly experienced more failure than success in their endeavors, and as a result, have learned to get attention and peer-group approval through misbehavior (Diller & Moule).

Culturally responsive teaching strategies are designed to help teachers avoid stereotypes and over-generalizations and become aware of the biases in their thinking and behavior (Cushner et al., 2006). According to Sleeter (2005), educators are cautioned against assuming that students from low-status groups develop poor self-concepts. Campbell (2005) stated demographic differences among staff and offenders—ethnicity, race, religion, gender, age, and nationality—may also influence correctional teaching and management conditions.

Wesley et al. (1993) suggested culturally responsive teaching aids frustrated teachers with classroom participation, and the ability to deliver lessons through effective instruction facilitation. This allowed the adult student responsibility for their own learning as they identify what they already know from life experiences. Wesley et al. suggested if teachers are effective culturally responsive teachers, they need to understand that the teacher's main role in culturally responsive teaching is to facilitate while allowing students to use their experience to resolve learning issues. Wesley et al. stated that in regard to prison, it is a complex learning environment; problems in the classroom can often be a result of curriculum or how it's being taught. Wesley et al. further stated that teachers should have educational experiences from various cultural perspectives, because prison classrooms are made up of different races as well as violent prison gangs.

Learning theory will aid teachers in creating atmosphere in which learners and instructors feel respected through learned experiences that includes learners perspectives, and values. According to Wesley et al. (1993), learning theory helps teachers break down stereotypes, make teaching and learning more accessible and equitable for a wide variety of students. By establishing an appropriate micro-culture within the prison classroom, it will provide a relaxing climate and space to work in their racially segregated minds. Teachers who know and understand that these conditions exist acquire knowledge of the culture that will allow the teacher to clarify attitudes and values that includes recognizing, accepting, and celebrating diversity as a fundamental fact and salient part of human life (Wesley et al., 1993). Correctional teachers need to become reflective practitioners. Reflective teachers apply observational, empirical, and analytical skills to monitor, evaluate, and revise their own teaching practices. They develop awareness of their own cultural perspective, thus gaining insight into the cultural assumptions underlying their expectations, beliefs, and behavior (Wesley et al., 1993).

This chapter examined complex skills that require knowledge and the cultural understanding that evolve over time from cross-cultural interpersonal experiences. Wesley et al (1993) suggested that correctional teachers need to become effective cross-cultural communicators. Effective cross-cultural communication skills help teachers create a classroom environment that encourages good int erpersonal relationships. This important interpersonal skill requires an understanding of the interrelationship between language and cultural meaning.

Chapter 3

METHODODLOGY

Research Design

The purpose of this project is to design a handbook that will help improve the teaching strategies of adult prison educational programs. The teaching strategies will be based on culturally responsive teaching as described in the literature. The research design consists of an ethnographic case study. The data collected and analyzed in this chapter are gathered from different sources. First, a seven-question survey was administered to 180 students. In addition, the school administrator and two teachers were interviewed. The researcher also played a key role as participant observer.

Setting of the Project

The project was developed to serve the teaching staff in correctional institutions in California. Many different types of programs fall under the rubric of CDC education. Many facilities offer grade-appropriate academic course work that address basic skill deficits, earn high school credits, earn the GED, and/or vocational preparation. This program helps parolees within a controlled prison environment to understand substance abuse and recovery using curriculum that includes the cycle of addiction. The process of recovery, stress management, healthy relationships, and relapse prevention. Additionally, these programs emphasize the development of pro-social behaviors and life skills.

The program operates five days a week, seven hours a day, and 284 days out of the year. Phase I curriculum consisted of drug recovery, Phase II consisted of family related issues, and Phase III dealt with employment and interview techniques. The teachers employed in the educational program have educational backgrounds. Most teachers in this program have a K-12 credential, and have taught in public schools. Teachers who come from a traditional teaching environment may experience cultural shock once they step onto the prison yard. Classrooms are located inside the prison dorms where inmates live. The restrooms are located inside the classroom, with no walls or doors blocking the teachers view of the restroom. Teachers may face constant interruption during lecture including CO's escorting new inmates to their beds, and dragging mattresses across the floor. There are many other disruptions that must take place because of CDC procurers.

California is famous across the country thanks to a country song about a prison recorded by Johnny Cash in 1956. The city's rich history actually began more than a century earlier with California's great Gold Rush and arrival of the railroad. Gold was first discovered along the south bank of the American River in the area known as Negro Bar. The discovery led to massive gold mining operations, as well as a need for rail service. The teaching faculty at California Prison consists of 13 teachers; eight fulltime teachers and five part-time teachers. Teachers by ethnicity are as follows; White (54%), Blacks (38%), Hispanics (eight percent).

Population and Sample

As mentioned above, a seven question survey was administered to 180 students. In addition, the school administrator and two teachers were interviewed. The researcher also played a key role as participant observer. The program administrator was chosen for this project because he was the only administrator at the facility. His duties included planning, organizing, controlling and directing student programs and services operations, as well as education program compliance. The administrator established and maintained related time-lines and priorities. This included the direction and monitoring activities to assure student education programs and assigned functions comply with established standards, requirements, laws, codes, regulations, policies and procedures.

Teachers who were chosen for this project had less than two years of teaching experience. Teachers work one-on-one with parolees (students) to develop a personalized Community Transition Plan. Specific risk areas are addressed throughout the plan that also includes educational and employment strategies and other vital resources. The ethnicity and cultural background of the teacher might play a critical role when developing a student's transition plan. As opposed to trained teachers, those who are not trained in adult education may not have empirical understanding of how incarceration can influence the inmate's economic viability. When inmates return home, the prospects for employment are bleak. Of the many challenges facing inmates, none is as challenging as finding shelter and community resources. Small pockets of homeless programs are scattered throughout the urban communities. These communities are the back-drop of the minority teacher's experience. Many untrained teachers will struggle with providing services to poverty stricken inmates.

All students currently in custody volunteered to participate in the project. Students demonstrate success by obtaining a GED, increasing basic skills, completing a 90-day substance abuse education program, completing competency based certificates in computer applications, and completing steps to getting a job. The student population consists of

180 students; Whites (60%), Blacks (15%), Hispanics (14%), and Others (eleven percent). As a participant observer, the author is a fulltime adult education teacher and acting program administrator.

Data Collection

The student survey consisted of seven questions ranging on a scale from one thru five, with one, not at all agree and five, almost always agree. The questionnaire measures a student's commitment to continuous learning and understanding of culturally responsive teaching. Answering the survey requires the students to make a judgment about the extent to which key elements are in place in the classroom.

During the project, as a participant observer, the author observed classrooms for teacher and student-teacher interaction during class session. The segment of the observation includes a maximum of 60 minutes, 15 minutes for teacher's observation and 15 minutes for student observation. The first 15 minutes focus on the entire classroom, looking at both student groups and the number of students off task; not doing class work or out of the classroom. The teacher was observed for management, interaction, or socialization. The remaining 15 minutes were devoted to observing either the teacher or target student.

The interview questions for the teachers and administrator were different. The two teachers answered eight interview questions that were based on teaching background, classroom experience, classroom management, and teaching style. The administrator questions were based on his experience working in prisons, measuring the success of the education programs and students.

Data Analysis

Analysis of Data

A survey was administered to 180 students. In addition, the school administrator and two teachers were interviewed. The researcher also played a key role as participant observer. The results from the student surveys will be presented in such order, followed by the interviews of the administrator and two teachers. As participant observer, the researcher will also discuss his observations.

The following is a presentation of the survey and interview results. The survey results by question are presented first, followed by the interview results.

Question 1 of the survey asked if the learning objectives were clear, understandable, and realistic. After reviewing the data, beginning with question one, it was evident that one hundred twenty seven students or 70% of those surveyed, agreed a great deal that the learning objectives were clear and understandable. Forty-five or 25% of the students indicated that they agreed somewhat, that the objectives were clear. It must also be noted that one percent of the students surveyed indicated that the objectives were not clear at all.

Question 2 asked what learning strategies and resources seemed reasonable, appropriate, and efficient. One hundred and eleven (62%), of the students felt that the learning strategies and resources seem reasonable and appropriate. There was some indication by ninety-three or 52% of the surveyed students agreed a great deal, that the learning strategies and resources seem reasonable, appropriate, and efficient. Only eighteen or one percent of the students indicated that the learning strategies were not appropriate.

Question 3 asked if the teacher helps the student exploit their own experiences as resources for learning. One hundred and eight or 60% of the students agreed a great deal that the teachers helped them exploit their own experiences. Forty-five (25%) indicated that the teacher did not help them exploit the experiences very much. Eighteen or one percent of the survey group indicated the teachers did not at all help them exploit their own experiences.

Question 4 asked if the teacher involved the students in developing mutually acceptable methods for measuring progress. Ninety-three or 52% of the students indicated that teachers almost always involve them in developing mutually acceptable methods for measuring progress. It was also indicated that thirty or 20% agreed that teachers did not involve students very much in developing ways to measure their progress.

Forty-five or 25% of the surveyed students indicated that they somewhat felt teachers did not involve them the in the measurement process, while 36 students or two percent of the students felt that the teachers did not involve them at all in the methods for measuring progress.

Question 5 asked if the teacher helped the students develop and apply procedures for self-evaluation. Ninety three or 52% of those students surveyed, agreed a great deal that teachers helped them with self-evaluation. Also, ninety students or 50% agreed teachers almost always help students develop and apply procedures for self-evaluation. While 36 students or two percent of the students surveyed, indicated that the teachers did not help them develop and apply procedures for self evaluation.

Question 6 asked if the teacher helped the students to apply new learning to their own experience. One hundred twenty four or 69% of the students strongly indicated almost always or agreed a great deal that teachers help them apply new learning to their own experience. Twenty-one or twelve percent indicated teachers somewhat helped students to apply new learning to their own experience. It must also be noted that fifty four or three percent of the survey students indicated they were not helped with applying learning to their own experiences.

Question 7 asked the student to share their thinking about options available in the design of learning experiences. One hundred twenty four or 69% of the students surveyed agreed that almost always teachers shared their thinking about options available in the design of learning experiences. Ninety or five percent of the students surveyed indicated that teachers somewhat shared their thinking about options in design of learning experiences.

The results of the interview of the school administrator are discussed below, followed by the results of the teacher interviews.

Question 1 asked the administrator how they would describe their culture and backgrounds. The responses was African American populations, when asked about other possible cultural groups within his family he mentions that he has Native American and French, but he only identified with the Black culture.

Question 2 asked the administrator how they got involved with working in corrections. The program administrator stated before becoming an administrator he worked with the juvenile probation population as a counselor. He is inspired when he sees students succeed, because inmates have so many failures throughout their lives.

Question 3 asked the administrator what was the best aspect of their job. The administrator stated being involved with corrections allows him to see firsthand, students growing beyond self-defeating beliefs that have plagued them most of their lives.

Question 4 asked administrators what were the worst aspects of their job. The administrator stated it is that students in the program are forced to attend the school. Regardless of the reason they attend the program, the negative attitudes and criminal behavior are the first things teachers encounter. Because of the defensive behavior, teachers find it difficult and labor intensive during instruction.

Question 5 asked what their thoughts were on how humans learn. The response was that all students learn differently. Teachers at this program used different techniques so that the student can absorb the information they receive, whether they learn through, kinetics, lectures, or audio. These techniques are incorporated into the daily lesson.

Question 6 asked what they have found to be the key factors in adult learning. The administrator stated andragogy practices, teaching techniques and repetition.

Question 7 asked what methods the teacher used to measure success in their program. Success in the program was measured by the time it takes students to return to prison. Inmates are notoriously known for returning to prison within thirty or forty days. With the help of this drug treatment program students stay out of prison as long as six months or more.

Question 8 asked what strategies they used to build relationships with students being in a punitive system of prison. The administrator stated that it was important for the student to learn and improve on who they are as a person, and to know their own limitations. Students' relationships with their teachers were important because students from different backgrounds are taught by teachers with different backgrounds and different races.

Question 1 asked the teachers if learning objectives were clear, understandable, and realistic. Both teachers agreed that the learning objectives were clear, understandable and realistic. Teachers learning objectives described what students will learn, and directed students toward closing the gap between where they are academically and the level they want to achieve.

Question 2 asked if learning strategies and resources seemed reasonable, appropriate and efficient. Teachers stated their learning strategies were usually pluralistic and required student interaction and group work. They provided learning contracts as a means for negotiating reconciliation between expectations and the learner's needs and interests.

Question 3 asked if the teacher helps the student exploit their own experiences as resources for learning. The teachers stated they gear their presentation of their own experiences as resources for learning through the use of such techniques as discussions, role playing case method.

Question 4 asked the teacher if they involved the students in developing mutually acceptable methods for measuring progress. Teachers felt they helped the students develop and apply procedures for self-evaluation. This was accomplished by sharing and becoming a participant learner, as well as a member of the group expressing their own view as well as deep personal feelings.

Question 5 asked the teacher if they helped the students develop and apply procedures for self-evaluation. Most of the students felt the teachers helped them with self-evaluation. Two percent of the group labeled other indicated the teacher did not help them develop and apply procedures for self-evaluation.

Question 6 asked if the teacher helped the students to apply new learning to their own experience. Teachers believed they exposed students to new possibilities of self-fulfillment throughout the classroom experience with an open non-authoritarian atmosphere that will be conducive to learning initiative and creativity.

Question 7 asked teachers if they shared their thoughts about options available in the design of learning experiences. Teachers stated they used methods that involved the students in deciding their learning options together as a class, using cooperation by guiding and directing students in a natural manner.

Following are the observations of the researcher as a participant observer. During the first 15 minutes, focus was on the entire classroom; looking at both student groups and the number of students off task, and not doing class work or workout of the classroom. The author noticed that inmates would leave class to lie down on their beds, or go outside to play basketball during class hour. Teachers would have to disrupt class and coach the inmate back to his seat. This type of disruption was frequent during the observation process and teachers seemed to have little control of the problem or any methods for solving students disappearing from class. The teachers followed prison disciplinary action, by filing the proper forms, but the corrections department responded slowly are not at all to the teacher's request. This type of non-responsiveness significantly causes more failure than success in classroom. As a result, power is given to inmates when their bad behavior goes unchallenged. Inmates were responding in aggressive ways towards teachers such as talking while teachers were trying to instruct the class, wearing head phones in class, doing other work such as drawing pictures or writing letters to loved ones. This unmanaged behavior increases their negative attitudes toward education, and provides more reasons why correction educational programs are failing and cause inmates to return home in worse mental condition than before they went to prison.

Therefore, how can correctional teaching and management conditions in educational programs function properly under these conditions? CDC education needs to create a structure designed to ensure program integrity and effectiveness that involves the formulation of written policies and procedures and the determination of who will be responsible for the operation of the programs. This pattern of failure has prevented many inmates from having respect for themselves and others, creating more imaginary walls and obstacles to rehabilitation, including culturally responsive teaching and learning in adult prison educational programs.

Findings

Several major findings emerged from the data presented above. The following are the major findings:

1. Teachers reported that they involve students in a mutual process of formulating learning objectives in which the needs of students are met.

2. Teachers stated they gear their presentation towards their own experiences as resources for learning through the use of such techniques as discussions, and role playing methods. Although all teachers were not trained in culturally responsive teaching, 108 or 60% of the students felt that the teachers helped them exploit their own learning experiences.

3. One hundred twenty four, 69% of the students surveyed, agreed that almost always, teachers shared their thinking about options available in the design of learning experiences. Ninety, or five percent of the students surveyed, indicated that teachers somewhat shared their thinking about options in design of learning experiences.

4. Ninety-three or 52% of those students surveyed agreed a great deal that teachers helped them with self-evaluation. Also ninety students or 50% agreed teachers almost always help students develop and apply procedures for self-evaluation. While 36

students or two percent of the students surveyed indicated that the teachers did not help them develop and apply procedures for self evaluation.

5.   Ninety-three or 52% of the student's indication that teacher's almost always involve them in developing mutually acceptable methods for measuring progress.

Teachers believed that they exposed students to new possibilities of self-fulfillment, by involving students in a mutual process of formulating learning objectives in which the needs of students are met. The data showed that 126 (70%) of the student population agreed that teachers did not involve students in developing ways to measure their progress. Data showed that 36 or two percent of the teachers stated they did not involve them at all in the methods for measuring progress. They felt their culture and the process by which they learned best was not included in the learning experience. Forty-five (25%) of the students indicated that they somewhat felt teachers did not involve them in they can measurement their own progress. Overall, the teachers are doing an effective teaching job as indicated by 108 (60%) of the students agreed that the teachers help them exploit their own learning experiences. These findings are particularly encouraging, given that the majority of the teachers were not trained to teach in adult prison educational programs.

Overall, teacher and students' attitudes vary about classroom interaction. The teachers stated they gear their presentation of their own experiences as resources for learning through the use of such techniques as discussions, role playing case method. Teachers also believed that they exposed students to new possibilities of self-fulfillment, stating they involve students in a mutual process of formulating learning objectives in which the needs of students are met. The data showed that 126 (70%) of students agreed with the teacher, stating they shared their experiences and that it helped with self-evaluation. However, 36 (two percent) of the students surveyed indicated that the teachers did not help them develop and apply procedures for self evaluation.

Interpretation

Campbell (2005) suggested that self-evaluation for a correctional student is very important because self-evaluation forces a person to judge themselve before making judgment about others. Self-evaluation helps students know themselves, gives them control over how they will react in harsh correctional conditions may influence correctional teaching and management conditions. Ninety-three or 52% of those students surveyed, agreed a great deal that teachers helped them with self-evaluation. Also ninety students or 50% agreed teachers almost always help students develop and apply procedures for self-evaluation.

In culturally responsive teaching, styles should be modified to allow variability, active participation, and novelty in learning to allow multi-cultural education to be used as a yard stick to measure relevance, and effectiveness of teaching and communication styles, (Campbell, 2005). One hundred twenty four or 69% of the students strongly indicated almost always or agreed a great deal that teachers help them apply new learning to their own experience. Twenty-one or twelve percent indicated teachers somewhat helped students to apply new learning to their own experience. It must so be noted that fifty-four or three percent of the students indicated they were not helped with applying learning to their own experiences. Teachers should work hard to create the kind of classroom environment that critical thought. In such classrooms, students feel respected and had a certain degree of trust, because students cannot function at higher levels of cognitive activity when their anxiety level is high. Culturally responsive teaching enables students to be better human beings and more successful learners (Campbell, 2005).

Richards (2007) stated the teaching and learning system cannot waive the teachers' contribution, and the personal human contact between the student and teacher. One hundred twenty four or 69% of the students surveyed, agreed that almost always, teachers shared their thinking about options available in the design of learning experiences. Ninety or five percent of the students surveyed, indicated that teachers somewhat shared their thinking about options in design of learning experiences. Teachers believe they exposed students to new possibilities of self-fulfillment throughout the classroom experience with an open non-authoritarian atmosphere that will be conducive to learning initiative and creativity.

Muffoletto and Horton (2007) suggested that learning theory is of course, at the center of all educational programs. In regards to prison, it is a complex learning environment and problems in the classroom can often be the result of the subject, and how the teacher presents the subject. The administrator suggested that all students learn differently, and teachers at this program use different techniques so that the student can absorb the information they receive, whether they learn through, kinetics, lectures, or audio. These techniques are incorporated into the daily lesson. It was evident that one hundred twenty seven or 70% of students surveyed, agreed a great deal that the learning objectives were clear and understandable, while forty-five or 25% of the students indicated that they agreed somewhat that the objectives were clear. It must also be noted that one percent of the students surveyed indicated that the objectives were not clear at all.

Mayes et al. (2007) suggested students like to see a representation of themselves standing in front of the classroom. Having a multicultural staff acts as a reinforcer to help students identify with the material that is being presented. That is why it is an important element in accounting for human learning as the concept of secondary rein forcers. One hundred twenty four (69%) of the students surveyed, agreed that almost always, teachers shared their thinking about options available in the design of learning experiences. Ninety (five percent) of the students indicated that teachers somewhat shared their thinking about options in design of learning experiences.

Therefore, it is important that teachers begin their lesson where they are most comfortable, but teachers should remember to include learners' perspectives and values (Spronken-Smith. 2005). One hundred twenty four (69%) of the students strongly indicated they almost always or agreed a great deal that teachers help them apply new learning to their own experience. Twenty-one or twelve percent indicated teachers somewhat helped students to apply new learning to their own experience. It must also be noted that fifty-four (three percent) of the students indicated they were not helped with new learning experiences.

The interpretation of the data shows culturally responsive teaching styles should be modified to allow variability, and to be used as a yardstick to measure relevance, and effectiveness of teaching and communication styles. While twenty-one (twelve percent) indicated teachers believed they helped students apply new learning to their own experience, it must so be noted that fifty-four (three percent) of the students indicated they were not helped with applying learning to their own experiences. The data acknowledges that there is some disagreement between students' understanding of how the information is received and how the teachers are translating the information. Teachers believe they exposed students to new possibilities of self-fulfillment throughout the classroom experience with an open non authoritarian atmosphere that will be conductive to learning initiative and creativity. However, it must so be note that fifty-four (three percent) of the students indicated they were not helped with applying learning to their own experiences.

Description of the Project

The purpose of this project is to design a handbook that will help improve the teaching strategies of adult literacy prison educational programs that can be used as a reference manual. To experience the full effect of a culturally responsive teaching intervention, teachers were given an in-service training from a skilled facilitator; the creator of this project. Three in-service workshops were held in the months of February and March, 2009. Once the first in-service was completed, the facilitator conducted a classroom observation of each teacher. The following week there was additional in-service to follow up on the findings of the classroom observation.

Based on the findings of the students and teachers, Folsom Prison Educational Programs should consider implementing this process as one way to decrease student's misdirection and increase teacher effectiveness in the classroom. Their capacity to improve and develop as continuously improving learning communities could adopt this model as one method for achieving student's goals.

To experience the full effect of culturally responsive teaching, a handbook was developed that will help improve the teaching strategies of adult literacy prison educational programs that can be used as a reference manual. Teachers who had less than two years of teaching experience were chosen for this project. The ethnicity and their cultural background of the teacher played a critical role when developing a student's transition plan. Small pockets of homeless programs are scattered throughout the urban communities; these communities are the back-drop of minority teachers' experience. At the beginning of the classroom observation, three in-service workshops were halted and the first in-service was completed. The facilitator conducted a classroom observation of each teacher. The following week, there was an additional in-service to follow up on the findings of the classroom observation. The capacity to improve and develop as continuously improving learning communities is the purpose of this model as one method for achieving student's goals.

Summary

The purpose of this project is to design a handbook that will help improve the teaching strategies of adult prison educational programs that can be used as a reference manual. The problems encountered while developing this manual were lack of research done on the topic, and finding correctional sites that demonstrated program accomplishment. Other problems included obtaining the participation and support of key decision-makers. It is necessary to foster team development with both the prison policy makers and the working group to insure accountability. The involvement of prison policy makers ensures the accountability and careful direction of the planning process.

The research design consists of an ethnographic case study. A survey was administered to 180 students to measure academic efficacy, and teacher expectations and involvement in education process. In addition, two teachers, and the program administrator were interviewed. The survey design was employed for the systematic observation of teachers and students in a classroom setting. The collection of data for student surveys was conducted during class sessions because it helped control the collection methods once surveys were completed.

The teaching and student population at California Prison Educational Program consisted of 13 teachers; eight full-time teachers and five part time teachers. Teachers by ethnicity were White (54%), Blacks (38%), and Hispanics (eight percent). The student population consisted of 180 students; White (60%), Blacks (15%), Hispanics (14%), and Others (eleven percent).

The project was developed to serve the teaching staff in correctional institutions in California. Inmates in educational programs run by department of corrections. Data analysis and finding were computed for all questions, which respondents rated using a scale of agree to disagree. These ratings were added together to create findings for learning and effective teaching. Individual surveys and interview questions were compared and contrasted, and differences were found in the way teachers believe they teach compared to how students receive and process the information.

Findings from the data showed that teachers reported they involve students in formulating learning objectives in which the needs of students are met. Teachers did well in this area of their classroom instruction with 108 students agreeing that the teachers help them with explore new learning experiences. However, there were areas of classroom instruction that teachers did not perform up to the educational standard. Eighteen students indicated that they needed help with learning strategies and they felt the teaching methods that were used were not appropriate for their style of learning.

Self-evaluation helps students know themselves gives them control over how they will react in harsh correctional conditions may influence correctional teaching and management conditions. Self-evaluation is very important in correctional classrooms. Teachers did well where it counts as the results of the student survey, indicating ninety-three students agreed that teachers helped them with self-evaluation. Also, ninety students agreed that teachers helped students develop and apply procedures for self-evaluation. These are very pleasing results, because they indicated that teachers understand the importance of a student's self-worth that creates effectiveness of teaching and communication styles (Campbell, 2005). When teachers work hard to create a good classroom environment, students cannot function at higher levels of cognitive activity when their anxiety level is high. Culturally responsive teaching enables students to be better human beings and more successful learners (Campbell, 2005).

Teachers must use techniques so that the student can absorb the information they receive, whether they learn through, kinetics, lectures, or audio. These techniques are incorporated into the daily lesson. Seventy percent of those surveyed made a point of how well teachers made objectives clear and understandable. Students had positive experiences when teachers shared their thinking about options available in the design of learning experiences as indicated by ninety students. Therefore, teachers should begin their lesson where they are most comfortable (Spronken-Smith, 2005). Data shows culturally responsive teaching styles should be modified so they can help the fifty students with applying learning to their own experiences. The data acknowledges that there is some disagreement between students' understanding of how the information is received and how the teachers are translating the information.

Chapter 4

SUMMARY, CONCLUSIONS AND RECOMMENDATIONS

Summary

The purpose of this project is to develop a handbook to assist teachers with classroom management and effective communication while working at adult prison education programs. Knowledge and understanding of other cultures, racial, and ethnic groups, expose teachers to the values, beliefs, customs, and behaviors of other people. It encourages students to explore their own cultural and ethnic heritage, and how culture influences the way they see themselves and others. Understanding culture nurtures appreciation of diversity as a valuable human resource.

During the project classroom observation, it was observed that some of the teachers did not feel comfortable in their multicultural prison

80

classroom, correctional officers would disrupt the class, remove students and strip search them, and then return them to class causing cognitive dissonances in the classroom and learning would come to a halt. This manual is to give teachers tools to address disparities in the correctional classroom. Majority of prospective teachers in California State Prison educational Programs are white while a majority of the students are minority. Meanwhile, the increase of minority inmates has caused a culture mismatch in correctional education programs. This manual can be used as a guide for teachers, especially those who are not highly acculturated, to navigate the complex application and entry procedures that teaching programs typically require. Also, providing a challenge to feel comfortable, safe, and welcome in a monoculture environment that is not their own.

The development and dissemination of high-quality culturally responsive teaching materials are intended for widespread program improvement and replication. The long-term benefits of the project are at least twofold. First, prison institutions that adopt project materials will broaden access to culture learning opportunities for students and increase student services for individuals with learning disabilities. Second, correctional institutions will be able to work as a team with teaching staff. This project represents a major attempt to reform persistent problems in correctional education using known strategies of culturally responsive teaching, and learning theory in the correctional education system itself. The results will be immediately useable throughout the county, it is expected that adoption and implementation rates will be significant.

The problems encountered while developing this manual was lack of research done on the topic, and finding correctional sites that demonstrate program accomplishment. Other problems included obtaining the participation and support of key decision-makers. It is necessary to foster team development with both the prison policy makers and the working group to insure accountability. The involvement of prison policy-makers ensures the accountability and careful direction of the planning process.

The project's conceptual framework was based on the review of the following literature: Correctional Institutions Teaching and Management Conditions, Culturally Responsive Teaching and Learning Theory. There are strong links between correctional institutions teaching and management conditions that determine the success or failure of prison education programs (Mayes et al., 2007). When a solid structure is put into place, it has the potential for counteracting problems created by teachers who are not trained to work in a correctional setting. Management conditions in correctional classrooms can be physical and psychological. COs operating in crisis mode continue to function in that mode even when the situation does not demand it, disrupting the learning process and collaboration between custody staff and education staff (Campbell, 2005). This is where teachers could make the difference by helping inmates get off the repetitive cycle of incarceration, and overcome some of the psychological influences and effects of the institution. Teachers who choose to work in adult prison educational programs need education that helps them deal with inmates, and knowledge that enriches their understanding of domestic educational policy.

Therefore, how can correctional teaching and management conditions in educational programs function properly under these conditions? Correctional officers (CO's) assigned to educational programs should have special training in social work, and psychology as a component of the internal organization (Campbell, 2005). Creation of structure designed to ensure program integrity and effectiveness involves the formulation of written policies and procedures, and the determination of who will be responsible for the operation of the programs. Campbell stated internal collaboration encouraged employees to become more invested in the success of correctional educational programs, and they also have a better understanding of the programs goals, and benefits of both the correctional organization and the educational department.

Leaders who take advantage of collaborative opportunities provide openings for employees to become more actively engaged in the organization. Positive attitudes towards prisoners are important in securing the effectiveness of various correctional rehabilitation programs and the successful reintegration of prisoners after release (Kjelsberg et al., 2005).

In learning theory, the teaching and learning system compliment the teacher's contribution, and the personal human contact between the student and teacher. Learning theory helps the teacher break down stereotypes, and improve the identification of self in the realm of another person's world. Learning theory helps teachers to make learning more accessible and equitable for a wide variety of students (Gay, 2000). The students' ability and personality, psychological and sociological process, accompany a process of change. Learning theory confronts educational issues at both ends of the teaching and learning spectrum, and can make a class run smooth with the least classroom disruption. There is no single formula for conducting a class successfully, because the task is influenced by multiple conditions that vary from one place and time to another (Mayes et al., 2007). Those conditions include the number of students in the class and their characteristics, the instructor's traits, the nature of the learning tasks, the available teaching facilities. The core premise of learning style is that individual learner preferences will lead to learners being less effective in learning situations that require them to leave the comfort of their preferred learning strategies and styles. That is, people can learn how to learn differently from ways they naturally prefer (Thomas, 2006). Although no single existing book would serve as a comprehensive learning style textbook for use in teacher education programs, journal articles would provide sufficient coverage of the current state of cultural learning styles, theory and research, to improve considerably, the teaching style in prison education programs (Smith, 1998).

Culturally responsive teaching enables students to be better human beings and more successful learners. Students must believe they can succeed in learning tasks and have motivation to persevere. This can be done through attribution retraining, providing resources and personal assistance, modeling positive self-efficacy beliefs, and celebrating individual and collective accomplishments (Gay, 2000). Empowering education is a critical-democratic andragogy for self and social change. It approaches individual growth as an active, cooperative, and social process, because the self and society create each other. The goals of this andragogy are to relate personal growth to public life, to develop strong skills, academic knowledge, habits of inquiry, and critical curiosity about society, power, inequality, and change (Gay, 2000).

Culturally responsive teaching does not incorporate traditional educational practices with respect to students of color. It appreciates the existing strengths and accomplishments of all students and develops them further in instruction. It provides more opportunities for students to participate in cooperative learning and can be provided in the classroom (Gay, 2000).

Culturally responsive teaching is liberating, it guides students in understanding that no single version of 'truth' is total and permanent. It does not solely prescribe to mainstream ways of knowing. The validation, information, and pride it generates are both psychologically and intellectually liberating. Other improved achievements can include clear and insightful thinking, more caring, concerned, and humane interpersonal skills, better understanding of interconnections among individual, local, national, ethnic, global, and human identities, and acceptance of knowledge as something to be continuously shared, critiqued, revised, and renewed (Gay, 2000). Keating (2007) states teaching adults inmates can be either energizing, and self actualizing, or exhausting and frustrating. Culturally responsive teaching aids teachers with frustration, classroom participation, and the ability to deliver lessons through effective instruction facilitation. This gives the adult student responsibility for their own learning as they identify what they already know from life experiences. In regard to prisons, it is a complex learning environment. Problems in the classroom can often be a result of curriculum, and are closed institutions in which control is the primary concern and questioning authority is not tolerated. Cultural disconnects are often found within multicultural classrooms when teachers lack cultural competence and knowledge (Wesley et al., 1993). Teaching is just one of the many talents teachers must master in order to work in a prison classroom. Knowledge of culturally responsive teaching will aid teachers when students return to class after being search and stripped by CO's, or after a violent situation had occurred. After experiencing those situations, inmates often get frustrated and unreachable. Teachers should have educational experiences from various cultural perspectives, because prison classrooms are made up of different races, as well as violent prison gangs (Spronken-Smith, 2005).

The project was developed as a possible model for the state prison system, with the data was collected at one of the prisons in Northern California. The teaching and student population at California Prison Educational Program consisted of 13 teachers; eight full-time teachers and five part time teachers. Teachers by ethnicity were White (54%), Blacks (38%), and Hispanics (eight percent). The student population consisted of 180 students; White (60%), Blacks (15%), Hispanics (14%), and Others (eleven percent).

The research design consists of an ethnographic case study. A survey was administered to 180 students to measure academic efficacy, and teacher's expectations and involvement in education process. In addition, two teachers and the program administrator were interviewed. The survey design was employed for the systematic observation of teachers and students in a classroom setting. The collection of data for student's surveys was conducted during class sessions because it helped control the collection methods once surveys were completed. institutions in California. Inmates in educational programs are run by the Department of Corrections. Data analysis and findings were computed for all questions, which respondents rated using a scale of agree to disagree. These ratings were added together to create findings for learning and effective teaching. Individual surveys and interview questions were compared and contrasted, and differences were found in the way teachers believe they teach compared to how students receive and process the information.

Findings from the data showed teachers reported that they involve students in formulating learning objectives in which the needs of students are met. Teachers did well in this area of their classroom instruction with 108 students who agreed that the teachers helped them to explore new learning experiences. However, there were areas of classroom instruction where teachers did not perform up to the educational standard. Eighteen students indicated that they needed help with learning strategies and they felt the teaching methods that were used were not appropriate for their style of learning.

Self-evaluation helps students know themselves, gives them control over how they will react in harsh, correctional conditions, and might influence correctional teaching and management conditions. Self-evaluation is very important in correctional classrooms. Teachers did well where it counts, as the results of the student survey indicated ninety-three students agreed that teachers helped them with self-evaluation. Also, ninety students agreed that teachers helped them to develop and apply procedures for self-evaluation. These are very pleasing results because they indicated that teachers understand the importance of a student's self-worth and that it creates effectiveness of teaching and communication styles (Campbell, 2005. When teachers work hard to create a good classroom environment, students cannot function at higher levels of cognitive activity when their anxiety level is high. Culturally responsive teaching enables students to be better human beings and more successful learners (Campbell, 2005).

Teachers must use techniques so that the student can absorb the information they receive, whether they learn through, kinetics, lectures, or audio. These are techniques that are incorporated into the daily lesson. Seventy percent of those surveyed made a point of how well teachers made objectives clear and understandable. Students had positive experiences when teachers shared their thinking about options available in the design of learning experiences as indicated by ninety students. Therefore, teachers should begin their lesson where they are most comfortable (Spronken-Smith, 2005). Data shows culturally responsive teaching styles should be modified so that it can help the students with applying learning to their own experiences. The data acknowledges that there is some disagreement between students' understanding of how the the information.

Conclusions

The following conclusions emerged from the development and implementation of the project. First, teachers and students attitudes vary about classroom interaction. Teachers state that they gear their presentation of their own experiences as resources for learning, through the use of such techniques as discussions and role-playing methods. Second, teachers also believe that they expose students to new possibilities of self-fulfillment. Both teachers state they involve students in a mutual process of formulating learning objectives in which the needs of students are met. The data showed that students strongly agree that that they share their experiences and help them with self evaluation. Third, 36 or two percent of the students surveyed indicated that the teachers did not help them develop and apply procedures for self evaluation. Overall, the teachers are doing an effective teaching job, as a majority of the students agreed that the teachers help them to exploit their own learning experiences. These findings are particularly encouraging, given that the majority of the teachers were not trained to teach in adult prison educational programs. There is some disagreement between students understanding how the information is received and how the teachers are translating the information. Fourth, teachers believed they exposed students to new possibilities of self-fulfillment throughout the classroom experience with an open non-authoritarian atmosphere that will be conducive to learning initiative and creativity. However, it must be noted that fifty-four or three percent of the students indicated they were not helped with applying learning to their own experiences.

Recommendations

The whole teaching model provides a systematic design framework for the teacher to follow, and lends itself to the practical work of designing a prison educational training program. This learning model can be used at adult levels of education that will inform teachers lacking the knowledge of how to teach in adult prison educational programs. Learning theory forces the teachers to ask the question, what are the barriers to succeeding as a teacher in adult prison education programs? Learning in prison education programs occurs as the individual interacts with the positive teaching environment created by the teacher. Learning skills include learning from instructions, and assigned learning tasks created from learning activities.

In adult education, it is recommended that self-direct learning activities include how to manage the management conditions in the prison classroom, how to improve the learning experience, and how to take learning action. In culturally responsive teaching, effective adult learning uses the understanding of individual differences to tailor adult learning experiences. Learning experiences include tailoring the lesson plan to apply core principles to fit adult learners and their learning preferences, and use students' understanding of differences to expand the goal of learning experiences. These methods should be used to improve how teachers manage their classes and teach effectively. Rigorous evaluation and tracking of interaction between the teacher and student would have to be in place to help determine what works best with different types of offenders and to enable the program to be slowly refined.

Policies that relate to inmate movement like going to the restroom and being punished if they do not return to class in a timely manner only reinforces the students belief that it is okay to miss class because no one cares. This research has provided the framework for an evaluation to be put in place. If teachers are held to quality standards that encompass educational performance and are provided with necessary resources to teach, long term benefits will emerge in adult prison educational programs.

APPENDICES

Appendix A

HUMAN SUBJECTS APPROVAL REVIEW FORMS

1. Which of the following is this application for? **Semester Dec Year 2008. (EDLP) 250**

2. Does this project use members of any protected class? (This includes minors, prisoners, pregnant women, fetuses, elderly, patients of hospitals or mental facilities, or any person legally unable to give consent.) **YES**

3. Is this project exempt according to university standards? (Exempt research is that data collection carried out in an established course on the effectiveness of instructional techniques; observational research of adults that does not allow individual participants to be identified; a review of pre-existing anonymous records or survey; an evaluation of a public service program). **No**

4. Does this research pose any physical or Psychological ham to subjects? (Note: Studies that use deception are considered by IRB rules to pose psychological harm.) **No**

5. Does this research pose any physical or psychological harm to the research? If yes, please explain. **No**

6. Describe who will participate in this research as subjects.

    a. **Teachers working for Contra Costa Office of Education with less than two years of teaching experience in the education field,**

    b. **Inmates at Folsom Prison that are participating in the adult education program.**

    c. **Parents of inmates incarcerated at Folsom State Prison that are enrolled in the educational program.**

7. From what source will participates be selected?

Teachers that work in the adult prison education program. Inmates participating in the adult prison education program. Parents of inmates in the adult prison education program.

8. How will participates be recruited or selected (e.g., what inducements, if any will be offered)?

Teachers will be recruited during weekly in-service training, Inmates will be recruited during independent study hours, and parents will be recruited through phone or (direct) personal contact.

9. By what criteria will participates be selected?

Teachers working for the prison education program with less than two years teaching experience. Inmates participating in the adult prison education program and parents of inmates in the adult education program.

10. Describe how informed consent will be obtained from the subjects. **Attach a copy of the consent form you will use.** If a signed written consent will not be obtained, explain what you will do instead and why. (See CPSH Policy Manual, Appendix **B**, for examples of consent forms and a list of requirements. Policy Manual can be found at Http://www. caus.edu/rsp/HumanSubjects.htm.)

Teachers:

Teachers will be given an in-service about the Human Subject project during weekly staff development training. After the in-service training teachers will be asked if they would like to volunteer to participate in the survey, if the teachers consent to participate in the survey, they will be asked to read, complete, and sign the consent form, turning it into the interviewee before completing the survey.

Students:

During class the project will be explained to the students in detail, students will be informed of the purpose of the project and what the project will accomplish, after the in-service students will be offered a chance to volunteer to participate in the project. Before students can participate in the project they must read, complete, and sign a consent form and hand the form back to the interviewer before he can begin the filling out the survey.

Parents:

Parents will be given a detail explanation of the purpose of the project, and the goal of the project. After the in-service, parents will be offered a chance to volunteer to participate in the project by completing a survey. Before the survey can be completed, parents must read, complete and sign a consent form and hand it back to the interviewer.

How will subjects' rights to privacy and safety are protected? (See level of Risk in policy manual.

No names will be on the surveys, all surveys will be destroyed (shredded) once surveys are documented and recorded in the aggregate.

Summarize the studies or project's purpose, design, and procedures. (Do not attach lengthy grant proposals,

The purpose of this project is to study instructional practices useful in improving the academic achievement of all students, teaching methods in prison adult educational programs, and develop exemplary culturally responsive teaching. The research aims to examine and improve efforts aimed at building the teachers capacity to continue improvement on teaching strategies used and understanding of cultural responsive teaching. The project will arm teachers with the ability to effectively use cultural responsive teaching methods to increase students' knowledge and increase the desire for learning.

What is the purpose of the study or project?

The purpose of this project is to study instructional practices useful in improving the teaching methods and develop exemplary culturally responsive teaching. The research aims to examine and improve the impact of different levels and understanding of cultural responsive teaching.

Describe the research design that will be used.

The research design for EDLP 250 Cohort Project is a series of questions about the adult learning environment and how it is characterized by physical comfort, mutual trust and respect,

mutual helpfulness, freedom of expression. These experimental design questions allow some measure of statistical certainty that outcomes are due to adult education teaching strategies rather than other prison initiatives to which inmates (students) might have been exposed. This design include three sub designs; one for teachers, one for students, and one for parents of inmates involved in this project.

Described the data that will be collected (i.e., participant opinions, test scores, performance measures, etc.

Interview design is a data collection process in which all participations answer questions related to culturally responsive teaching. Survey questions will be deployed in the spring of 2009 Cohort semester. Teachers, Students, and is Community members (family with incarcerated members) will answer seven to fourteen questions about instructional strategies that hold promise for improving culturally responsive teaching.

Describe procedures for collection of data.

Teachers, students and parents methods of collecting the surveys will be the same method, to ensure data is collected systematically. Once the survey is completed, the survey will be collected immediately after the interview.

Describe the content of any tests, questionnaires, interviews, etc in the research.

Teacher Design (survey) was based on knowledge of culturally responsive teaching.

Collective Professional Capacity

School/family/ Connections

Shared Goals for learning

Effective Teaching

Student Design (survey) was based on students experience with their teacher, and whether the feels.

The learner perceives the goals of a learning experience to be their goals.

The learner accepts a share of the responsibility for planning and operating a learning experience.

The learners have as sense of progress toward their goals.

Parent surveys ask questions base on prior education experiences, with the list of questions related to teaching in adult education.

In your experience what has been some of the instructional delivery problems.

Human's beings have a natural potentiality for learning.

Presentation equals learning.

Evaluation is education and education is evaluation.

Much significant learning is acquired through doing.

Talking all aspects of this research into consideration, do you consider the study to be exempt "no risk?" **No risk. There will not be any physical risk.**

Appendix B

INTERVIEW PROTOCOL

Administrator Interview

1. How would describe your culture background?

2. How did you get into working with the prison population?

3. What is the best aspect of your job?

4. What are the worst aspects of your job?

5. What are your general thoughts on how humans learn?

6. What have you found to be the key factors in adult learning?

7. What makes your adult education program successful?

8. What methods do you use to measure success in your program?

9. What strategies do you use to build relationships with students that
    are in a punitive system of prison?

Teacher Interview Questions

1. Please describe your teaching background and experience?

2. Describe the method you use to check for student understanding?

3. How does lesson plans guild your teaching?

4. What teaching aides do you use?

5. To what extent do you take into account different learning styles?

6. How does the ethnicity of a student factor into the design of the lesson?

7. Do you believe that learning is culturally relative, to which the learner belongs may affect learning? Why or why not?

8. Do you believe the learner's abilities are important, and provisions have to be made for slower and more rapid learner? Why?

Student Interview Questions

1. Please describe the classes your attending

2. Please describe the process you use to reflect on the progress you have had while in the prison education program.

3. In class do you feel that the teacher communicates effectively with you?

4. Does the teacher provide solutions and help you move closer toward your goals with new ideals.

5. What method does the teacher use to insure that you understand the lesson?

6. To what extent does the teacher take into account the learning styles of the student?

7. Do you have any comments are questions for me?

Parent Interview Questions

Culturally Responsive Teaching in Adult Prison educational Programs

1. Adults orientation to learning is life centered:

   a. Not at all

   b. Not Very much

   c. Some what

   d. A great deal

   e. Almost always Very much

2. Adults are motivated to learn as they experience needs and interests that learning satisfies.

   a. Not at all

   b. Not very much

   c. Some what

   d. A great deal

   e. Almost always

3. Experience is the richest source for adult's learning.

   a. Not at all

   b. Not very much

   c. Some what

   d. A great deal

   e. Almost always

4. Adults have a deep need to be self-directing.

   a. Not at all

   b. Not very much

   c. Somewhat

   d. A great deal

   e. Almost always

5. Individual differences among people increase with age.

   a. Not at all

   b. Not very much

   c. Somewhat

   d. A great deal

   e. Almost always

Community Member Interview Questions

1. Please describe your position in the community.

2. How important do you feel it is for a teacher to evaluate the effectiveness of their lesson?

3. How important do you feel it is for the teacher to make changes for improvement?

4. To what extent should a teacher modify the design so subsequent lesson to improve the lesson.

5. To what extent should a teacher take into account the learning styles of the various students when designing a lesson?

6. Do you have any questions for me?

Appendix C

THE PROJECT: CULTURALLY RESPONSIVE TEACHING IN ADULT PRISONS: AN EDUCATIONAL PROGRAM

One of the major differences between traditional classroom instruction and prison educational program is the amount of face-to-face contact students have with their teacher and students. Once students leave class they return to the dorm where they live with their classmates, 24 hours a day, seven days a week. In this type of setting their learning becomes a social process, and the support of teachers and classmates can be an important element of the learning that occurs. Most teachers may meet with their students only once or twice over an entire course, with the remainder of the communication occurring in the classroom.

Some students have little or no face-to-face contact with their teacher other than class time. This means students need to possess the 114 characteristics (e.g., independence, self-motivation, organization and study skills, etc.) that enable them to succeed outside the classroom environment. There are many ways to assess student's characteristics, ranging from questionnaires to informal interviews with students. Obviously, not all students are suited for prison programs; in prison education, one size definitely *does not* fit all. The more specific an programs description is of its goals, the more useful it will be.

The Purpose of this Document

This book is specifically for new correction educators. This book is on how to teach and communicate effectively with offenders in a correctional educational setting.

This book is also written with the intent to remind teachers of where it is they work and the dangers they face if they work outside the rules while working in a correctional setting. The majority of inmates in the criminal justice system are undereducated and systemically powerless, mostly the black and brown men and boys already failed by a nightmarishly bureaucratic urban education system for who prison intensifies powerlessness. A few inmates enter prison with education and a critique—and acting on the critique may be what landed them there. In the end, the argument for or against this book or that for prison education is not the point.

The point is there are learning opportunities for inmates in prisons. That is no salvo to the system of corrections, rather, that is what people do dream, create, grow against all odds and in the most horrifying circumstances. This wonderful accident of humanness does not, however, mitigate the unbearable conditions of prisons or the reasons they placed into them. What is needed is acute dual attention to structural sicknesses of our society regarding racism, sexism, and the classed system of economic inequity.

Hill (2008) stated the department's adult education system is based on the public school model. Each prison operates its education program as an individual school composed of academic, vocational, and life skills instruction. Because of repetitive reentry and exit of inmates from prison, CDCR organizes classes on a model that provides an individual, self-paced program for each inmate.

In order for adult education teachers to be effective while working in California Department of Corrections, they should begin with students' prior knowledge, even if that understanding includes some misunderstanding, yielding to conceptual change as the goal.

Guidelines for Teacher-Inmate Learner Relationships

You are a role model for your learners. How you think about a subject will affect your learners' attitudes toward it. If you represent science as difficult, mathematics as boring, or history as a collection of facts, that is how your learners will view them.

You can limit your learners' access to important subject matter by the social organization you create in the classroom. Ability grouping, tracking, and competitive learning arrangements can limit learners' access to important knowledge and generalizations.

The style of leadership you assume in the classroom (authoritarian, laissez faire, democratic) or the type of power you exercise (expert, referent, legitimate, coercive, reward) can affect the willingness of culturally different learners to engage in subject matter learning tasks. If you want your learners to explore problems and ideas with others, consider how your own behavior and the relationships you establish with learners inhibit or promote such cooperation.

Guidelines for Learner-Subject Matter Relationships

Recognize that some inmates have certain attitudes, beliefs, and values about other cultural that have been acquired from their parents, peer group, and society at large. Many students have racial-stereotyped beliefs about people like inferior or superior status that are acquired during their environment.

Be aware of these beliefs and be prepared to represent subjects such as math and science in ways that bridge or confront the perceptions of your learners.

Remember that inmates' prior experiences with education may have been limited. Try convincing them that they can improve their ability in these subjects. Teach the subjects in ways that overcome these attributions.

Guidelines for Teacher-Subject Matter Relationships:

Recognize your own racial-stereotyped beliefs about certain cultural.

Teach your subject in ways that overcome the negative attributions regarding ability that race relations.

Use various examples and ways of representing your subject that do not reinforce racial stereotypes. For example, curriculum materials and teaching activities on the lesson of power should depict competent models of all cultural.

Objective	*Strategy*	*Learning Activity*
Establishing classroom pluralism. How do I create or affirm a learning atmosphere in Which participants feel respected and free to speak out	Multidimensional sharing	Have participants form small groups and share a topic they value within their cultural or social background
	Collaborative learning	Participants brainstorm triggers, or incidents that they find very challenging to them. Have students lists these on the board
Developing attitude: How do I create or affirm a favorable disposition toward learning through personal relevance and choice?	Make the learning activity exciting and an irresistible invitation to Learn	Students shares a method they used effectively to respond to one of the challenges listed on the board. Have groups reportchoosing one person as speaker and one student circles response those that mostly apply to them, invite the class to continue to share their ideals.

Enhancing meaning: How do I create engaging and challenging learning experiences that include learner perspectives and experience?	Use a variety of presentation styles to convey different concepts	Teacher uses an overhead, power point, black board and handouts to explain rules; uses brain storming exercise to aide in cooperative learning.
	Student critical thinking	The teacher asks the students to think of feelings and attitudes they have about their peers and to culturally respectful
Engendering competence: How do I create or affirm an understanding that students have effectively learned something that they value and perceive as authentic to their real world?	Activity assessment	Students examine what worked and did not work during this exercise, and what parts can they use in life.

Guidelines for Teacher-Learner Relationships

Remember that you are a role model for your learners. Do not communicate racial stereotypes about occupations and subjects during informal conversations with learners.

Teach group learning in ways that promote racially-free attitudes and beliefs about subject matter, occupations, and recreational activities.

Methods for Teaching in Adult Prison Educational Programs

There are many principles associated with adult learning. A compilation of these principles is detailed below.

- Instructors of adult learners need to keep in mind that they should:
- Present new information if it is meaningful and practical. If the learner sees no connection between the job/course and the activities, that person will very likely lose interest and not succeed in the class.
- Present only one idea or concept at a time. Show how one step progresses to the next. Use feedback/frequent summarization.

Keep the summaries of completed activities alive and strong as reinforcement.

- Practice learning as a self-activity.
- If they prefer to learn on their own, see if this is possible in the course without sacrificing in-class activities and their benefits.

Speaking and Listening

1. While communicating with inmates ask questions to clarify meaning, often times inmates will use slang terms. Teachers must demonstrate effective listening skills and respond appropriately to listener feedback.

2. Beware of using voice and body language appropriately and effectively, provide useful input and feedback using (peer editing, group discussion, classroom participation, etc.)

3. Respond appropriately to students, opinions, recognize that adults learn have prior life learning when they enter the classroom. Use hands-on experiences whenever possible, ones which parallel their work environment. Some adults learn better in groups, because this creates cohesion among them and their peers.

Student Expectations

1. Recognize self-esteem.

2. Employ strategies to deal with anger

3. Manage stress

4. Get to class on time analyzing and utilize time management strategies.

5. Explore and connect personal values and their impact on choices.

6. Create awareness of the emotional self.\

7. Examine learning process and practice the skills necessary for success.

8. Use methods to resolve conflict resolution.

9. Clarify the definition of assertiveness

10. Analyze the reasons for your bias and develop the ability to resolve it daily.

11. Identify issues around all forms of prejudice and practice non-discriminatory interpersonal relationships.

12. Investigate the various types of relationships and interaction they have with others

13. Practice developing positive relationships, including effective communication.

14. Look closely at diversity of relationships and cultures, and practice in daily life skills.

Teaching begins with students' prior knowledge, even if that understanding includes some misunderstanding, and conceptual change must be the goal.	The skills, knowledge, values and abilities that students bring to the classroom are fundamental factors related to learning. Teachers should weaken the inmates mind, open his eyes, rid him of what causes fear of learning and complexes he already has. Give them support and eliminate their inhibitions about education. Present information in a manner that permits mastery. This means "bit-size chunks" of information rather than everything in one huge swoop. Make the material relevant, as close to the actual requirements of that person's job. Add a little "spice to their life" by giving them some degree of options and flexibility in their assignments.
Know that culturally responsive teaching is empowering.	Inmates may take your kindness the wrong way. If you are uncomfortable about a request of the inmate you should consult your supervisor or correctional supervisor.

	Inmates base their whole reality on respect. Due to the unstable living conditions, and stress in prison dorms. Sometime inmates bring the stress from the dorms into the classroom and are often quick to react negative to the smallest put down.
Have knowledge of how to teach and work with inmates.

Never bring in anything for a specific inmate.

Never talk down to inmates.

Don't accept anything from inmates. | Teachers should not accept anything from inmates. This could create problems when it comes time for disciplinary actions, are it could result in sexual harassment. |
| Rational: Help the learner to want to perform the skill. | Use a simple story reflecting learner's problem and culture.

Video vignette reflecting learner's problem culture

Discuss past events |

Model; Show the learner how to perform the skill	Specify the response that makes the skill. Demonstrate each response. Describe each response orally during enactment.
Independent practice	Practice through games. Practice through role play.
Teachers are committed to students and their learning.	Some teachers have good intentions about being academically unjust and discriminatory toward ethnically and racially different students. Others understand that being aware of cultural differences in classroom interactions. But, good intentions and awareness are not enough to bring about changes needed in prison education programs.
Noticing inmate's individual culture is important.	In adult education, by accepting the validity of students' cultural socialization and prior experiences will help to reverse achievement trends.

LEARNING STYLE	TEACHING TECHNIQUES
Visual-Language: This is the student who learns well from seeing words in books, on the chalkboard, charts or workbooks. He/she may write words down that are given orally in order to learn by seeing them on paper. He or she remembers and uses information better if it has been read.	This student will benefit from a variety of books, pamphlets, and written materials on several levels of difficulty. Given some time alone with a book, he or she may learn more than in class. Make sure important information has been given on paper, or that he or she takes notes if you want this student to remember specific information.
Visual-Numerical: This student has to see numbers on the board, in a book, or on paper in order to work with them. He or she is more likely to remember and understand math facts if he or she has seen them. He or she does not seem to need as much oral explanation	This student will benefit from worksheets, workbooks, and texts. Give a variety of written materials and allow time to study it. In playing games and being involved in activities with numbers and number problems, make sure they are visible, printed numbers, not oral games and activities. Important data should be given on paper.

LEARNING STYLE	TEACHING TECHNIQUES
Auditory-Language: This is the student who learns from hearing words spoken. You may hear him or her vocalizing or see the lips or throat move as he or she reads, particularly when striving to understand new material. He or she will be more capable of understanding and remembering words or facts that have been learned by hearing	This student will benefit from hearing audio tapes, rote oral practice, lecture, or a class discussion. He or she may benefit from using a tape recorder to make tapes to listen to later, by teaching another student, or conversing with the teacher. Groups of two or more, games or interaction activities provide the sounds of words being spoken that are so important to this student.
Social-Group: This student strives to study with at least one other student and he or she will not get as much done alone. He or she values others' ideas and preferences. Group interaction increases his or her learning and later recognition of facts. Socializing is important to this student.	This student needs to do important learning with someone else. The stimulation of the group may be more important at certain times in the learning process than at others and you may be able to facilitate the timing for this student.

LEARNING STYLE	TEACHING TECHNIQUES
Expressive Oral: This student prefers to tell what he or she knows. He or she talks fluently, comfortably, and clearly. The teacher may find that this learner knows more than written tests show. He or she is probably less shy than others about giving reports or talking to the teacher or classmates. The muscular coordination involved in writing may be difficult for this learner. Organizing and putting thoughts on paper may be too slow and tedious a task for this student.	Al low this student to make oral reports instead of written ones. Whether in conference, small group or large, evaluate him or her more by what is said rather than what is written. Reports can be on tape, to save class time. Demand a minimum of written work, but a good quality so he or she will not be ignorant of the basics of composition and legibility. Grammar can be corrected orally but is best done at another time.
Expressiveness-Written: This student can write fluent essays and good answers on tests to show what he or she knows. He or she feels less comfortable, perhaps even stupid when oral answers are required. His or her thoughts are better organized on paper than when they are given orally.	This student needs to be allowed to write reports, keep notebooks and journals for credit, and take written tests for evaluation. Oral transactions should be under non-pressured conditions, perhaps even in a one-to-one conference.

REFERENCES

Barron, N. G., Grimm, N. M. & Gruber, S. (2006). *Social change in diverse teaching contexts: Touchy subjects and routine practices.* New York: Peter Lang.

Bartolome, L. (2008). *Ideologies in education; Unmasking the trap of teacher neutrality.* New York, NY: Peter Lang.

Benham, M. (January, 2005). National education association summit on Asian and Pacific Islander issues in education: Native Hawaiians, Pacific Islanders, and Filipinos. NEA Headquarters, Washington, DC.

Bjork, C., Johnston, K. & Ross, H. (2007). *Taking teaching seriously.* Boulder, CO: Paradigm Publishers.

Bryson, B. (2005). *Making multiculturalism, boundaries and meaning in US English departments.* Stanford, CA: Stanford University Press.

Campbell, N. M. (2005). *Correctional leadership competencies for the 21ˢᵗ century: Executives and senior-level leaders*. Washington, DC: US Dept of Justice, National Institute of Corrections.

Cartledge, G., Gardner, R. & Ford, D. (2009). *Diverse learners with exceptionalities. Culturally responsive teaching in the inclusive classroom*. Upper Saddle River, NJ: Person Education Inc,

Cole, M. (2006). *Education, equality and human rights: Issues of gender, 'race', Sexuality, disability and social class*. New York, NY: Routledge.

Cowdery, J. R., Ingling-Rogers, L., Morrow, L. & Wilson, V. A. (2007). *Building on student diversity: Profiles and activities*. Thousand Oaks, CA: Sage Publications.

Cushner, K., McClelland, A. & Safford, P. (2006). *Human diversity in education: An integrative approach*. New York, NY: McGraw Hill.

Diller, J. V. & Moule, J. (2005). *Cultural competence: A primer for educators*. Belmont, CA: Thomson/Wadsworth.

DiPaola & Hoy (2008). *Principals improving instruction, supervision, evaluation, and professional development*. Boston, MA: Pearson/Allyn and Bacon.

Donavant, B. W. (2008). The new, modern practice of adult education. Online instruction in a continuing professional education setting. *Adult Education Quarterly: A Journal of Research and Theory, 59*(3), 227-245.

Feistritzer, C. E. & Haar, C. K. (2008). *Alternate routes to teaching.* Upper Saddle River, NJ: Pearson/Merrill/Prentice Hall.

Galbraith, M. W. (2004). *Adult learning methods: A guide for effective instruction.* Malabar, FL: Krieger Publishing Company.

Gay, G. (2000). *Culturally responsive teaching: Theory, research, and practice.* New York: Teachers College Press.

Gillett, A., Hammond, A. & Martala-Lockett, M. (2009). *Inside track to writing academic essays.* Harlow: Longman.

Gouin R. (2009). An antiracist feminist analysis for the study of learning in social struggle. *Adult Education Quarterly, 59*(2), 158-175

Hoosain, R. & Salili, F. (2005). *Language in multicultural education. Research in multicultural education and international perspectives.* Greenwich, CT: Information Age Publishing.

Johnson, D. D., Johnson, B., Farenga, S. J. & Ness, D. (2005). *Trivializing teacher education: The accreditation squeeze.* Lanham, MD: Rowan & Littlefield Publishers, Inc.

Joshee, R. & Johnson, L. (2007). *Multicultural education policies in Canada and the United States.* Vancouver, BC: UBC Press.

Justice, L. M. (2006). *Clinical approaches to emergent literacy intervention.* Emergent and Early Literacy Series. San Diego, CA: Plural Publishing.

Keating, A. (2007). *Teaching transformation: Trans-cultural classroom dialogues.* New York, NY: Palgrave Macmillan.

Kember, D. & Gow, L. (1994). Orientations to teaching and their effect on the quality of student learning. *The Journal of Higher Education, 65*(1), 58-74.

Kjelsberg, E. S., Skoglund, T. H. & Rustad, A. B. (2007). Attitudes towards prisoners, as reported by prison inmates, prison employees and college students. *BMC Public Health,* 7.

Knowles, M. S., Holton, E. F. & Swanson, R. A. (2005). *The adult learner: The definitive classic in adult education and human resource development.* Amsterdam: Elsevier.

Kohler-Giancola, J., Grawitch, M. J. & Borchert, D. (2009). Dealing with the stress of college: A model for adult students. *Adult Education Quarterly: A Journal of Research and Theory, 59*(3), 246-263.

Kosnik, C., Beck, C., Freese, A. & Samaras, A. (2006). *Making a difference in teacher education through self study.* Dordrecht: Springer.

Li, G. & Beckett, G. H. (2006). *Strangers of the academy: Asian women scholars in higher education.* Sterling, VA: Stylus Publishing.

Lieb S. (Fall, 1991). Principles of adult learning: Adults as learners. South Mountain Community College, *Vision.*

Mayes, C., Cutri, R. M., Rogers, P. C. & Montero, F. (2007). *Understanding the whole student: Holistic multicultural education.* Lanham, MD: Rowan & Littlefield Education.

Michelli, N. M. & Keiser, D. L. (2005). *Teacher education for democracy and social justice*. New York: Routledge Farmer.

Moore, M. G. (1980). Independent study. In R. Boyd & J. Apps (Eds.), *Redefining the Discipline of Adult Education*, pp. 16-31. San Francisco, CA: Jossey-Bass.

Muffoletto, R. & Horton, J. (2007). *Multicultural education, the Internet, and the new media*. Media Education Culture Technology, Cresskill, NJ: Hampton Press.

Muth, B., Gehring, T., Puffer, M., Mayers, C., Kamusikiri, S. & Pressley, G. (2009). Janie Porter Barrett (1865-1948): Exemplary African American correctional educator. *Journal of Correctional Education: Official Publication of the Correctional Education Association, 60*(1), 31-51.

Nesbit, T. (2009). More words in edgeways: Rediscovering adult education, by J. Thompson. *Adult Education Quarterly, 59*(3), 271-273.

Pedersen P. (2004). *110 experiences for multicultural learning*. Washington, DC: American Psychological Association.

Peters-Davis, N. & Shultz, J. (2005). *Challenges of multicultural education: Teaching and taking diversity courses*. Boulder, CO: Paradigm Publishing.

Powell, R. G. & Caseau, D. (2004). *Classroom communication and diversity: Enhancing instructional practice.* LEA's communication series. Mahwah, NJ: L. Erlbaum Associates.

Presseisen, B. Z. (2008). *Teaching for intelligence.* Thousand Oaks, CA: Corwin Press.

Proefriedt, W. (2008). *High expectations: The cultural roots of standards reform in American education.* New York: Teachers College Press.

Richards, P. B. (2007). *Global issues in higher education.* New York: Nova Science.

Ryndak, D. L. (2006). *Teachers and learners in inclusive schools: A collection of readings.* Dubuque, IA: Kendall/Hunt Publishers.

Sandlin, J. A. & Walther, C. S. (2009). Complicated simplicity: Moral identity formation and social movement learning in the voluntary simplicity movement. *Adult Education Quarterly: A Journal of Research and Theory, 59*(4), 298-317.

Sleeter, C. E. (2005). *Un-standardizing curriculum; Multicultural teaching in the standards based classroom.* New York: Teacher College Press.

Sleeter, C. E. & Grant, C. A. (2003). *Making choices for multicultural education: Five approaches to race, class and gender.* New York: J. Wiley and Sons.

Smith, G. (1998). *Common sense about uncommon knowledge: The knowledge bases for diversity*. Washington, DC: AACTE.

Souryal, S. (2009). Deterring corruption by prison personnel: A principle-based perspective. *Prison Journal, 89*(1), 21-45.

Spronken-Smith, R. (2005). Implementing a problem-based learning approach for teaching research methods in geography. *Journal of Geography in Higher Education, 29*(2), 203-221.

Stengel, B. S. & Tom, A. R. (2006). *Moral matters: Five ways to develop the moral life of schools*. New York: Teachers College Press.

Suskie, L. & Banta, T. W. (2009). *Assessing student learning; A common sense guide* (2nd Ed.). San Francisco, CA: Jossey Bass.

Thomas, D. R. (2006). A general inductive approach for analyzing qualitative evaluation data. *American Journal of Evaluation, 27*(2), 237-246.

Thomas, R. G. & Thomas, R. M. (2008). *Effective teaching in correctional settings: Prisons, jails, juvenile centers, and alternative schools*. Springfield, IL: Charles C. Thomas Publishers.

Travis, J. (2005). *But they all come back. Facing the challenges of prisoner reentry*. Washington, DC: Urban Institute Press.

Weis, L. & Fine, M. (2005). *Beyond silenced voices: Class, race, and gender in United States schools*. SUNY series, frontiers in education. Albany, NY: State University of New York Press.

Weis, L., McCarthy, C. & Dimitradis, G. (2006). *Ideology, curriculum, and the new sociology of education: Revisiting the work of Michael Apple*. New York: Routledge.

Wesley, S., Rosenfeld, M. & Siins-Gunzenhauser, A. (1993). *Assessing the classroom performance of beginning teachers: Teachers' judgments of evaluation criteria*. Princeton, NJ: Educational Testing Service.

Wood, J. A., Russell, T. T., Wilson, B. & Ireton, E. J. (2005). *Teaching Latino students effective strategies for educating America's minorities*. Lewiston, NY: The Edwin Mellen Press.

CPSIA information can be obtained
at www.ICGtesting.com
Printed in the USA
LVHW030014190221
679483LV00034B/436

9 781450 086769